South Korea's Demographic Dividend

Echoes of the Past or Prologue to the Future?

Author
Elizabeth Hervey Stephen

CSIS | CENTER FOR STRATEGIC &
INTERNATIONAL STUDIES

ROWMAN & LITTLEFIELD
Lanham • Boulder • New York • London

Center for Strategic & International Studies
1616 Rhode Island Avenue, NW
Washington, DC 20036
202-887-0200 | www.csis.org

Published by Rowman & Littlefield
A wholly owned subsidiary of The Rowman & Littlefield Publishing
Group, Inc.
4501 Forbes Boulevard, Lanham, MD 20706
www.rowman.com

Unit A, Whitacre Mews, 26-34 Stannary Street, London SE114AB

ISBN 978-1-4422-8084-7 (hardcover)
ISBN 978-1-4422-8085-4 (paperback)
ISBN 978-1-4422-8086-1 (electronic)

The paper used in this publication meets the minimum requirements of
American National Standard for Information Sciences—Permanence
of Paper for Printed Library Materials, ANSI/NISO Z39.48-1992.

Center for Strategic & International Studies   Rowman & Littlefield
1616 Rhode Island Avenue, NW   4501 Forbes Boulevard
Washington, DC 20036   Lanham, MD 20706
202-887-0200 | www.csis.org   301-459-3366 | www.rowman.com

For Anne, friends, family, and mentors

Contents

ACKNOWLEDGMENTS

As with all major writing projects, it takes a village, and in this case, it has taken villages from shore to shore. This work was supported by the Academy of Korean Studies (Korean Studies Promotion Service) Grant funded by the Korean Government (Ministry of Education) (AKS-2010-DZZ-2102).

The person who has been most influential in every stage of this book has been my Georgetown University colleague and friend, Victor Cha. We have had the good fortune of being POSCO Fellows at the East-West Center in Honolulu, Hawai'i along with our other Georgetown colleagues, Michael Green and Christine Kim. Along with Ambassador Christopher Hill at the University of Denver we benefited greatly from having a Korean Lab, which brought an interdisciplinary approach to each of our research projects. Victor has been a source of intellectual support at all stages of this project. I thank all of my Georgetown colleagues on the Academy of Korean Studies (AKS) project, and Sang Jun Lee for his masterful administration of our five-year grant.

I also want to thank the East-West Center for hosting me not only during the POSCO Fellowship but during subsequent years as well. The space and collegial atmosphere were critical in the early stages of this project. Denny Roy, Nancy Lewis, Carolyn Eguchi, Andy Mason, Minja-Kim Choe, and Sang-Hyop Lee facilitated my research and provided valuable insights.

Georgetown University also provided key funding to support the writing of this book during the summers and provided research assistants throughout the years. The School of Foreign Service provided consistent support and the Graduate School of Arts and Sciences awarded me summer support for 2016. Carol Sargent provided excellent advice throughout the project.

I have worked with dedicated research assistants over the years and all of their work is reflected here. I wish to thank Peter Castagno, Emily Coccia, Caroline Egan, Katrina Kleck, Sookyung Koo, Kenneth Lee, Yaeseul Park, Rachel Ryu, and Kevin Sullivan. Their dedication to detail is shown in every table and every figure. D. Sanford Hesler assisted in the writing of the education section of Chapter 2.

I have been very fortunate to have had two strong mentors: Frank D. Bean while I was at the University of Texas at Austin and Ronald R. Rindfuss from the University of North Carolina at Chapel Hill. Ron and I had many stimulating conversations about every topic under the sun, and some of our last conversations took place in Busan, South Korea. I miss our conversations, but treasure that Ron is still a part of our lives. Frank Bean was instrumental in the writing and editing of the first and last chapter of this book, which were derived from a co-authored paper presented at the annual meeting of the Population Association of America meeting in April 2017.

I have been supported throughout this project by my friends far and near, but a few deserve special mention. Georganne O'Connor edited every word of this text, and cheerfully at that! My daily "conversations" with Leann Tigges sustained me, as did my less regular—but no less important—relationships with my support system in Washington, DC, Bald Head Island, NC, and all points in between. A special thanks to Paul Castagno for his good cheer and good times during the last revisions of this book.

During the time I have been writing this book my daughter, Anne, was pursuing her undergraduate degree at Kenyon College and then launched her postgraduate degree at Marquette University. I thank Anne for her patience and for being a great roommate in Hawai'i. My sister, Dianne Harper, and her family (Jim, Anne, and Erin) are constant sources of strength.

To every student, every friend, every colleague, both mentors, my family, Paul, and Anne, I thank you from the bottom of my heart.

1. DEMOGRAPHIC TRANSITIONS AND ECONOMIC DIVIDENDS: SOUTH KOREA AND THE ASIAN TIGERS

South Korea is often referred to as a success story: a country that has undergone rapid economic development. That vibrancy has been achieved in part by a demographic dividend, an additional boost to growth occurring during a window of time when a large percentage of a country's population is in the working ages as a result of low fertility and declining mortality (Bloom, Canning, and Sevilla 2003). During the apex of the demographic dividend there is also a relatively small dependent population owing to the percentage of the elderly cohort having not yet increased and the percentage of children having decreased. This allows working-age cohorts to amass savings at a rate previously unknown in that country, while at the same time increasing productivity. Despite these favorable circumstances, South Korea's elderly have not benefited much from the country's growth, necessitating a close examination of South Korea's development, the factors behind it, and a portrait of those left behind.

Our story begins more than a half-century ago when a small group of less developed countries began an unusual period of rapid economic growth. Eventually known as the Asian Tigers—Hong Kong, Singapore, South Korea, and Taiwan—these places mimicked the prior experience of Japan a decade earlier. Along with a second tier of countries (Malaysia, Thailand, and Indonesia) following close behind (Barro 1998), the Asian Tigers roared onto the world economic development stage, all showing stronger economic growth

2 Elizabeth Hervey Stephen

from 1960 to 1995 than countries in any other region in the world. These achievements were sufficiently unusual that they are often referred to as economic miracles (Barro 1998). By the late 1990s, however, the transformative and high per capita economic growth rates of these places, including South Korea's, had begun to slip, prompting confusion and concern in South Korea and other national governments about whether strong economic growth was coming to an end.

Over this same time span, social scientists were increasingly studying how much and in what ways changes in demography affected economic growth and vice versa (Abio et al. 2017; Kelley and Schmidt 2005; Williamson 2013). An important conclusion that emerged from this research was that population growth per se did not appear to be related to economic growth. In a classic study, Bloom and Williamson (1997) estimated that favorable changes in population dynamics accounted for 1.4 to 1.9 percentage points of annual per capita gross domestic product growth in East Asia during the period of 1965 to 1990, or about one-third of total economic growth for these countries.

From the late 1990s on, East Asian countries began to experience still further declines in fertility, raising concerns that the initial benefits of declining fertility perhaps might be disappearing or turning negative because of declines in the sizes of work forces and in some cases, even overall populations. For example, Japan's population reached 127.8 million persons in 2008 and declined to 126.7 million in 2016, with continued contraction likely in the foreseeable future (U.S. Census Bureau 2017). Even though relatively smaller non-working age populations may have initially helped foster South Korea's economic miracle, analysts and policymakers have started to worry that the smaller relative sizes of the subsequent working-age populations might be making it harder to sustain previously high economic growth rates. In addition to reexamining their macroeconomic policies, countries and researchers increasingly focused on what kinds of factors help to sustain economic growth, or at least cushion its decline. Given that drops in fertility persisted among the East Asian Tigers, policymakers wondered about what kinds of demographic changes and social policies might forestall or minimize any negative effects stemming from further fertility decline. This is nowhere more true than in the anomalous situation of South Korea, the focus of this book. Analysts increasingly suggested that forces such as rising education and its effect on productivity were substantially responsible for bringing about economic miracles in countries such as South Korea (Crespo Cuaresma, Lutz, and Sanderson 2014; Rentería et al. 2016). This notwithstanding, it remained the case that changes in national demographic structures, although perhaps only intermediate factors through which education and productivity exerted their effects on economic growth, have real consequences themselves. For example, increasing education levels, especially among women, may initially lead to lower fertility, which in turn results in a relative expansion of the working-age population. However, when such low fertility lasts for a long enough period of time, or even declines further, this eventually results in relatively fewer potential workers, a phenomenon that itself can act as a drag on economic growth. Thus, whatever the origins of changes in the age structure of populations, it is useful to assess the viability of social and other policies that might be adopted to prevent relative declines in the sizes of working-age populations or compensate for their effects.

The purpose of this book is to present such an assessment for South Korea and to determine if the economic benefits enjoyed as a result of declining fertility have been distributed uniformly through the population. In South Korea the benefits of rising economic growth have not benefitted the elderly nearly as much as they have the young. Nearly half (46 percent) of the elderly in South Korea live in relative poverty, which is the highest of any developed country and is approximately four times the Organization for Economic Cooperation and Development (OECD) average (OECD 2018). This highlights why it is important to assess whether and how future demographic and social policies in South Korea might be able to help cope with looming slowdowns in economic growth. To do this, we must not only delve into the demographic and socioeconomic drivers and consequences of economic growth but also their differential distributional consequences. In other words, it is useful for us to examine in more detail ideas about demographic transitions and their consequences.

FIRST AND SECOND DEMOGRAPHIC TRANSITIONS

Kirk (1996, 361) defined demographic transition theory (DTT) as follows: "Stripped to essentials it [DTT] states that societies that experience modernization progress from a pre-modern regime of high fertility and high mortality to a post-modern one in which both are low." An intermediary period of the demographic transition has been characterized by high rates of population growth as a result of declining mortality and the continuation of high fertility rates. Then as nations complete the demographic transition and exhibit low and stable rates of mortality and fertility, economic and public policy factors gain importance as determinants of the age structure of the population.

Two concepts have evolved from demographic transition theory both of which are particularly relevant for our analyses: the second demographic transition (SDT) and the concept of demographic dividends. Demographic transitions and demographic dividends—whether in their first or second phases—are related concepts but refer to differing phenomena in a population. The term second demographic transition (SDT) was coined by Lesthaeghe and van de Kaa (1986) and elaborated by van de Kaa (1987). Lesthaeghe and van de Kaa proposed that rising secular and individualistic viewpoints led to: (1) new living arrangements and higher levels of cohabitation, (2) postponement of marriage and parenthood, and (3) an increase in the share of births to unmarried couples. The characteristics of the SDT are now evident throughout Europe, including most Central European countries. There are critics of the SDT who argue that it is merely an extension of the first demographic transition; that the model does not explain behavior outside of Western Europe, Canada, and Australia; and/or that it is a secondary feature of the demographic transition rather than a transition in and of itself (Lesthaeghe

2010). Nevertheless, we find the conceptual underpinnings of the theory of interest in trying to explain changes in demographic behavior over time in East Asia, and specifically in South Korea.

THE SECOND DEMOGRAPHIC TRANSITION: AN ASIAN EXCEPTION OR VARIATION?

Coleman (2004, 12) described the second demographic transition:

> In essence the theory proposes that the new freedom of sexual behaviour, the diversity of forms of sexual partnership, and the relaxation of traditional norms and constraints observed in many developed societies since the 1960s, are intimately related and share common causes. They are held to be irreversible and likely to become universal. The new transition is made possible by parallel trends in further economic growth, intellectual emancipation through education and the concomitant ease of diffusion of ideas, especially reflected in the status of women.

Lesthaeghe and Neidert (2006) explored whether the United States was an exceptional case of the SDT since the total fertility rate has remained relatively high at just below replacement level, although there has been a rise in postponement of marriage and parenthood. They conclude that "the United States is a textbook example of the second demographic transition where immigration and higher immigrant fertility compensate for sub-replacement fertility of much of the native population" (Lesthaeghe and Neidert 2006, 694). They also state that the United States is not exceptional, rather that the United States is bipolar with regional differences. For instance, members of the conservative and religious right who are more likely to live in states such as Utah and regions of the South, Midwest, and the Great Plains align more closely with certain behaviors and are less likely to delay marriage and childbearing, and are more likely to have children within marriage, than those who identify with more left-leaning political viewpoints. Persons on the east and west coasts as well as persons from the less religious West

(Colorado, New Mexico, and Arizona) follow demographic behavior more akin to that of Europe with delayed marriage and childbearing, and higher levels of cohabitation and non-marital childbearing.

Asian countries are also experiencing the second demographic transition but I propose that Asia—and in particular East Asia—is the more exceptional case than the United States. The Asian pattern of marriage and childbearing within marriage is clearly deviant from that observed in most European countries and the United States. Lesthaeghe (2010, 225) argued that the theory allows for heterogeneity and that "the mixture of SDT ingredients may vary widely depending on context." In this chapter we explore what context allowed for elements of the SDT to be adopted in South Korea, while other elements or ingredients have not been embraced.

THE EAST ASIAN VARIATION

Over the past 20 years fertility levels have declined in East Asia, while being accompanied by delayed marriage and childbearing. In some aspects of demographic behavior, East Asian countries follow the European pattern of the SDT. For example, the mean age of marriage and childbearing for women in Taiwan, Japan, and South Korea are close to that of most of the selected European countries (Figure 1.1).

However, alternative forms of marriage, particularly cohabitation, have not become more popular in Asian countries—with the exception of the Philippines—as seen in Figure 1.2. In addition, children born outside of marriage is rare in the Asian countries as shown here (except for the Philippines, which is an economic outlier as well as a demographic outlier). McNicoll (2006) noted that the Philippines had a slow agrarian reform that led to the country having delayed manufacturing export opportunities, leaving the country with a slow economic growth pace and a relatively slow pace of fertility decline. The Philippines' trajectory has led to its outlier position among the highly successful East Asian economies.

As seen in Figure 1.3, the mean age at marriage for women is above age 25 for Taiwan, Japan, and South Korea, which is similar to that of the United States and selected European countries. The scat-

Figure I.I. Scatterplot of mean age at first birth by mean age at first marriage for women in selected countries, circa 2016

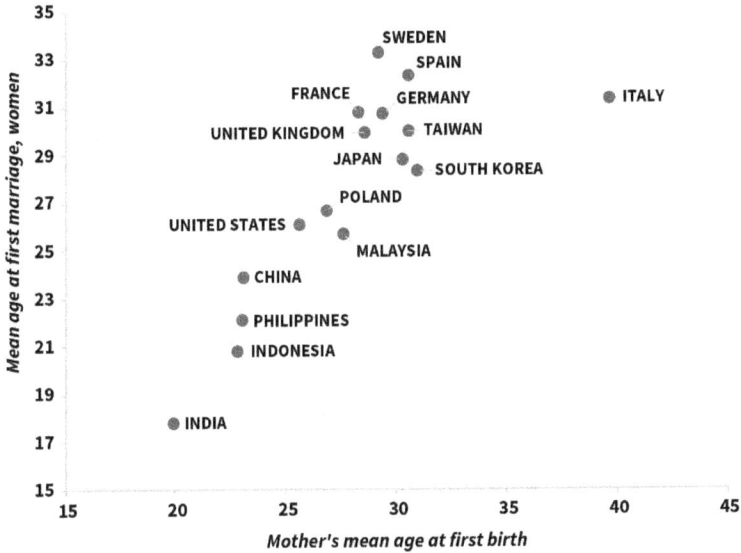

Sources: China: China Statistics Press (n.d.); European countries: EUROSTAT (2016); Malaysia: Department of Statistics (2015); Taiwan: Ministry of the Interior (2016); United States: U.S. Census Bureau (2017); all other countries: CIA (2014).

terplot reinforces the pattern that had also been observed in Figure I.2: the percentage of childbearing outside of marriage is very low in Asia—with the exception again of the Philippines. So while marriage is delayed in East Asia, the pattern of childbearing within marriage is in stark contrast to the United States and Europe. For example, in France and Sweden 53 and 55 percent of births, respectively, occur outside of marriage, while Taiwan has the highest percentage among the East Asian countries at 4 percent.

The question is what is the locus for the changes in marital behavior in East Asia and specifically in South Korea? Although analysts cite the shift to more individualistic and idealistic views along with a more secular society as the driving forces for the SDT in Europe, I argue that changes in demographic behavior in South Korea are a result of a shift away from Confucianism and a strong extended

Figure 1.2.   Scatterplot of percentage of births outside of marriage
by percentage of women cohabiting in selected
countries, circa 2016

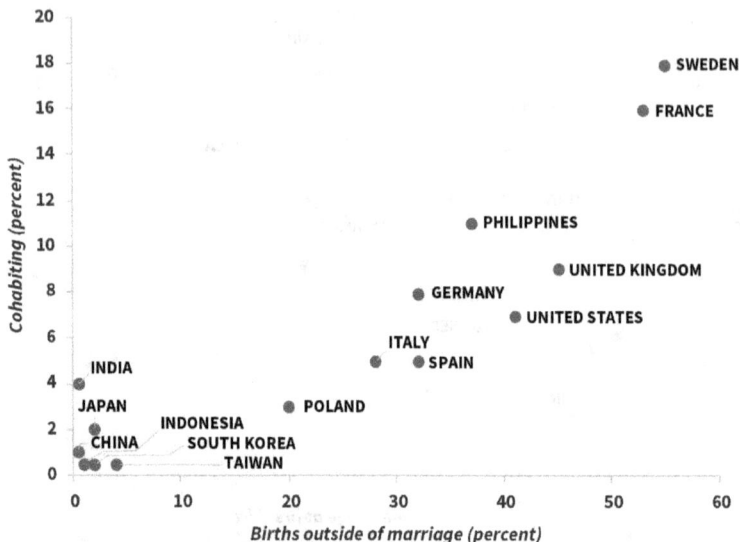

Sources: China: China Statistics Press (n.d.); European countries: EUROSTAT (2016);
Malaysia: Department of Statistics (2015); Taiwan: Ministry of the Interior (2016);
United States: U.S. Census Bureau (2017); all other countries: CIA (2014).

family network toward a more religious society. For the last two cen-
turies, Confucianism has been pervasive in every aspect of Korean
life. It centers the family as the fundamental unit of society and de-
termines hierarchical social relations. Confucianism in South Korea,
however, is a philosophy, a set of ethics and values, not a religion.

Organized religion, most specifically Christianity, came to South
Korea in the last 50 to 60 years. In 1962, 90 percent of Koreans reported no religious affiliation (Park and Cho 1995). Only 1 percent
of the Korean population was Christian in 1900, but by 2014, over a
fourth (29 percent) of the population reported being Christian
(Catholics, Protestants, and other denominations) (Connor 2014).
The majority of Korean Christians belong to Presbyterian, Meth-
odist, Baptist, and Pentecostal churches; Catholics have grown from

Figure 1.3.   Scatterplot of percentage of births outside of marriage by mean age at first marriage for women in selected countries, circa 2016

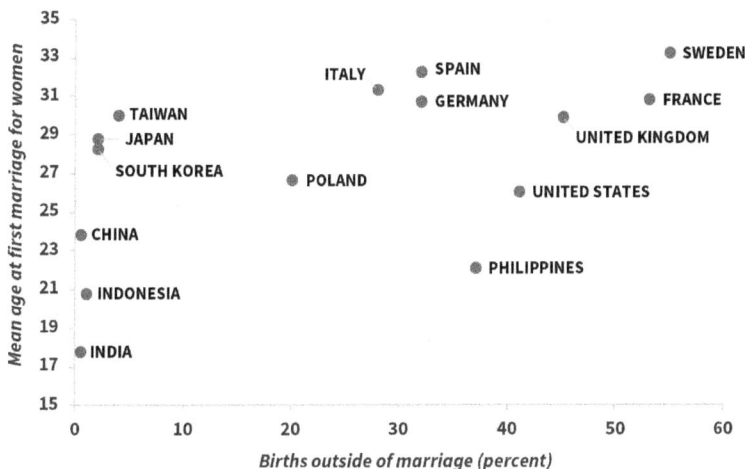

Sources: China: China Statistics Press (n.d.); European countries: EUROSTAT (2016); Malaysia: Department of Statistics (2015); Taiwan: Ministry of the Interior (2016); United States: U.S. Census Bureau (2017); all other countries: CIA (2014).

5 percent of the population in 1985 to 11 percent in 2005 (Connor 2014). The rise in Christianity began with the increasing role of the United States in the country following the Korean War. The association of American Christianity was a "source of strength and wealth" at a time when the country was rapidly urbanizing and newcomers to cities were looking for a social group and a new identity (Hazzan 2016). This rise in religiosity in South Korea is in direct contrast to the increased secularization of most of Europe. Just 5 percent of Swedes attend church on a regular basis, according to Statistics Sweden, although the Swedish Church (Svenska Kyrkan) reports 6.3 million members in a country of just under 10 million people ("Sweden 'Least Religious' Nation" 2015).

Another possible historical reason for the paucity of cohabitation and births outside of marriage in South Korea relates to primary and secondary marriages that once were allowed, particularly among noblemen. Secondary wives were subordinate to the primary wife, and children from the second marriage were not part of the father's lineage, which is so important in Confucian hierarchical family structure. Ravaneral et al. (1999) suggest that modern-day cohabitation is shunned in South Korea given the social stigma associated with secondary wives and their children.

Coleman (2004, 16) argues, "The underlying theory of the SDT posits radical ideational change made possible by economic progress." I argue, however, that ideational change to more secular societies in Europe explains the rise of the SDT while the movement to a more religious society in South Korea explains resistance toward cohabitation and childbearing outside of marriage. At the same time, economic development and expanding opportunities for women explain the rise in median age at marriage and childbearing. In South Korea, the combination of the increase in a Christian belief system overlain with Confucian values has led to a cementing of sequential life-course events such that childbearing follows marriage: an ordering that has eroded in most European countries.

DEMOGRAPHIC TRANSITION AND DIVIDENDS

Transformations in economic trends and population structures often result in subsequent social and economic changes (Casterline and Bongaarts 2017; Harper 2016). For example, what demographers call the demographic transition in many countries has led to relatively larger working-age cohorts that support relatively fewer dependents, thus generating what is often called a demographic "gift" or dividend (Williamson 2013). Several important processes produce such dividends. The first comprises rapid declines in mortality—especially infant mortality—from improvements in health care delivery and social/economic development. Second, drops in mortality induce reductions in fertility as a result of economic strains on larger families and increased availability of family planning. Third, economic growth results in less need for children to support parents as they age. This trifecta creates a window of economic opportunity where the size of the working-age population grows relative to the sizes of other age groups. This is due in part to the elderly population that is not yet disproportionately large. Thus, the resulting relatively large cohorts of workers lead to higher per capita incomes and boosts in economic growth, a result called the demographic dividend. These changes and increases in education can also lead to larger percentages of women participating in the formal labor market, further increasing per capita and household income.

But demographic dividends do not automatically persist as a consequence of age restructuring; sufficient policy measures must be in place to foster savings to sustain or even raise productivity and maintain the gains in per capita growth. Just as previous investments in education were important for demographic transitions (Crespo Cuaresma et al. 2014), additional measures to induce savings are important for sustaining demographic dividends (Rentería et al. 2016). Maintenance of dividends is not guaranteed, but rather, represents a bonus for the countries that adopt such policies. For the Asian Tigers that experienced demographic transitions, the beneficial period lasted as long as five or more decades. Consistently lower rates of fertility result in smaller working-age cohorts toward the end of demographic dividend periods; however, declines in mortality lead to increases in life expectancy and a higher proportion of elderly in the country. Thus, growth in per capita income slows and the economic boons associated with the first demographic dividend may be at risk of eroding.

Lee and Mason (2006) propose that a second demographic dividend can also emerge. The timing of the end of a first demographic transition and the onset of a second may vary, but as the authors argue, "The dividends are sequential: the first dividend begins first and comes to an end, and the second dividend begins somewhat later and continues indefinitely" (p. 16). The point at which the first dividend is positive is described by Mason and Lee (2006) as the point at which the effective number of producers is growing more rapidly than the effective number of consumers. Likewise, it can become negative when the number of dependents (young and especially elderly) increase relative to the size of the working-age population.

I argue, however, that a second dividend consists of the first one *not* coming to an end, but rather evolving into a new or second phase. This is possible if the population concentrated in the working ages has an incentive and ability to save and accumulate assets, particularly for cohorts anticipating an extended period of retirement. In short, the first dividend yields a transitory bonus, but this can continue, at least to an appreciable degree, when a portion of the first dividend is set aside for workers' retirement, thus reducing reliance on children for parental support. The first and second demographic dividends have been likened to "opposite sides of the same coin" (Mason and Lee 2006). But unlike the first demographic dividend, which results from working-age parents having fewer children, the second occurs when both the first dividend-producing generation and the next have accumulated enough wealth to substantially cover the anticipated costs of retirement. This second dividend does not saddle the smaller cohorts of offspring with intergenerational transfers to their elderly parents, which otherwise would potentially slow economic growth.

Even more so than with the first dividend, governments must put national strategic planning and policy measures in place for a country to maintain such economic boosts into and through a second phase. In particular, public policy measures to help support the elderly are necessary, especially when this population is increasing rapidly in relation to the total population. But care must also be taken not to implement transfer programs for the elderly that are so costly or large that economic growth is curtailed. At the same time, policies must be in place to sustain productivity, thus maintaining economic growth and sound financial systems (Lee, Mason, and Park 2012).

THE SOUTH KOREAN DEMOGRAPHIC DIVIDEND

The first demographic dividend in South Korea began in 1970/1971 and is traceable to President Park Chung-hee's policy reforms in the 1960s that opened the country to international trade and encouraged personal savings. A period of rapid economic growth ensued, influenced in no small measure by state interventionist policies that favored large industrial firms such as Hyundai and Samsung, which were given preferential trade treatment (Noland 2014). This authoritarian developmental governance approach emphasized a government-directed model whose implementation was aided by a rapidly urbanizing population and provided a workforce in the cities where the state-guided industries were located. One key for an economy to reap the advantages of a demographic dividend is to emphasize human capital to raise productivity, which, in the case of South Korea, was facilitated by two important factors: (1) favorable education policies developed in tandem with economic goals, and (2) large cohorts of young people.

Here I suggest that there were two parts to South Korea's demographic dividend when looking at social consequences as well as economic benefits. While the working-age population and children benefited from the demographic dividend, taken as a whole, South Korea's elderly population was bypassed as the dynamics of the demographic dividend unfolded, and have even been negatively affected. The older persons in this cohort (those born in or before 1952) lived through the Japanese occupation; all were alive for the civil war; and they all experienced the country's rapid industrialization. Moreover, many elderly have been constrained from participating in the modern industrial era because of low education levels and because of their low migration rates from rural to urban areas. This means that South Korea's elderly were unable to accumulate savings as a result of the demographic dividend and many have had no opportunity to participate in pension plans. As a result, poverty rates among the South Korean elderly are very high, a phenomenon exacerbated by declining family support and minimal government transfers. I return to this topic in Chapter 4 of this book.

The demographic dividend is not a guarantee, but rather a bonus for the countries that do capitalize on it. The Asian Tigers, particularly South Korea, benefited from large cohorts aged 15–64 from 1970 through 2010. As seen in Figure 1.4, this cohort, which in large part represents the labor force, grew from 55 percent of the Korean population between 1950 and 1970 to 70 percent in 1990 and reached

Figure 1.4.   Actual and projected percentage of total population
aged 15–64 for Japan, South Korea, and the United States,
1950–2050

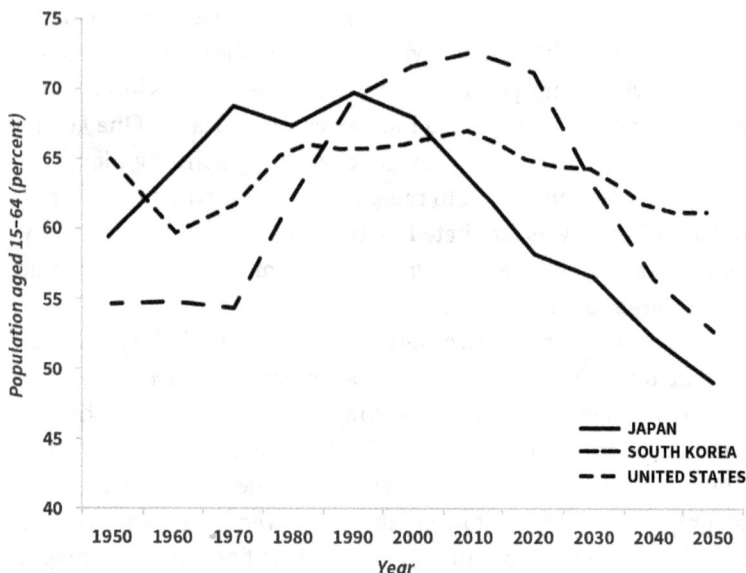

Source: U.S. Census Bureau (2017).

its apex at 73 percent in 2010. This age distribution favored South
Korea far more than it did in Japan and the United States, with this
advantage expected to continue until 2030.

A SECOND DEMOGRAPHIC DIVIDEND?

A second demographic dividend derives from increased life cycle
savings, which enables a longer retirement period and contributes
to capital accumulation and economic growth. The challenge for
South Korea is finding ways to provide a decent level of support for
the next generation of elderly without imposing a crushing burden
on the working population given the rapidly aging population. An
et al. (2011, 381) argue that, "whatever worked for Korean retirees

in the past will not work in the future." What are the prospects then for a second demographic dividend in South Korea? In spite of the projected low fertility continuing into the foreseeable future, which will result in a contraction of the labor force, Lee and Mason (2013) are optimistic about South Korea's ability to maximize human capital investment. They propose three critical factors that make this likely: (1) increased accumulation of wealth as a result of a larger elderly population, (2) increased life cycle savings for a longer period of post-retirement, and (3) declining child dependency. The authors admit that "heavy reliance on transfer systems in any form to meet old-age needs may short-circuit the effect of population aging on the demand for retirement wealth and the accumulation of assets and capital" (Lee and Mason 2013). But in analyses of Asian countries they have found that if one-third of the needs of elderly are met through transfers and two-thirds by assets, there is "substantial capital accumulation in a closed economy."

In essence, a successful economy heavily weighted by the elderly relies less on labor and more on capital. Historically familial transfers have had the greatest importance for Koreans; Lee and Mason (2013) are cautiously optimistic that the level of public transfers will expand to surpass that of familial transfers. Another key factor in their optimistic view of the future points to past and current spending on education and health. Lee and Mason propose that higher levels of education will increase productivity in the labor force, thereby offsetting the decrease in the number of working-age people. This combined with increased assets invested domestically will assist in tempering the falling support ratio. Other research supports a productivity hypothesis; a cross-national comparative analysis of panel data by Cutler et al. (1990) found that decreasing labor growth resulted in increasing labor productivity. This may seem counterintuitive, but Scarth (2002) argued that productivity could be enhanced by increased investment in human capital as labor becomes more scarce. In order to better determine the likelihood of a second demographic dividend in South Korea, there is also a need to take into account the demographic, behavioral, and economic consequences of what is termed the demographic transition: the shift from periods in a country of high mortality/high fertility rates to low mortality/low fertility rates.

What is often lost in the macro or aggregate discussions of the demographic dividend, however, is that it may be positive for some groups and negative or neutral for other groups. I argue that although the demographic dividend for the entire country of South Korea was positive and the effects have benefited the working-age population and children, the current elderly population has not benefited to the same extent and has been negatively affected. To put this into context, Chapter 2 examines factors that led to South Korea's tremendous economic success, including concurrent policy reforms and investment in human capital through education, which were key drivers of the first demographic dividend. We also examine obstacles for achieving a second demographic dividend. Crespo Cuaresma, et al. (2014, 299) have shown convincingly that national economic activity and productivity are a direct effect of improvements in educational attainment, or in other words that "a substantial portion of the demographic dividend is the educational dividend." To assess the effect of the educational dividend in South Korea, we examine in detail the changes in the education system from 1950 through the current time.

Chapters 3 and 4 of this book examine whether the SDT and the demographic dividend have been or are currently manifesting themselves in East Asian countries—and specifically South Korea—and posit explanations for the observed patterns. We consider each of the processes separately and then determine if the macro-level demographic structure of South Korea shows any evidence that the two concepts are related or reinforcing one another. Even within the working ages, however, not all groups have benefited equally as is illustrated by the interplay between societal forces and the economic structure of the country that have led to disparities. For instance, women in South Korea have been marginalized in the domestic and public spheres as a result of the hierarchical family structure supported by Confucianism and successive authoritarian military regimes that maintained laws and policies, which have been amended only recently.

In Chapter 4 we turn to the elderly population to determine why the demographic dividend bypassed them and ways that their economic plight has manifested itself as a health crisis. The transformation to the industrialized country of today, however, has come at societal costs. The elderly are living disproportionately in rural areas and many are experiencing the effects of the rapid change from co-residential stem (multigenerational) families to nuclear families at the same time the country has shifted from an agrarian to an industrial economy. Suicide rates for the South Korean elderly are the highest in the world, indicative of the social fractures evident for those left behind. How, and if, the second demographic dividend will benefit these age cohorts will depend upon a number of factors discussed in this chapter.

In Chapter 5 we offer policy options for South Korea to move forward in achieving a second demographic dividend and at the same time fostering social cohesion. The conclusion integrates the comprehensive analysis of the social and economic structure of the earlier chapters with concrete policy options for South Korea to benefit and continue its stellar economic progress and presents an analysis of the feasibility of various policy options and the present study's overall conclusions.

2. THE FIRST AND SECOND DEMOGRAPHIC DIVIDENDS IN SOUTH KOREA: PERFECT EXAMPLE OR PERFECT STORM?

South Korea experienced unparalleled economic growth in the latter half of the twentieth century. This chapter explores the drivers of this economic miracle in a country that in the mid-1950s was one of the poorest in the world. After independence from Japan in 1948 and in the mid-1950s, South Korean economic recovery and/or growth seemed a distant dream. The gross domestic product (GDP) per capita was US$155.60 in 1950, which was lower than that of the Cote d'Ivoire (US$157.20 GDP/per capita) (World Bank 2016). Over 60 percent of the Korean population lived below the absolute poverty level at the time (Adelman 2014). Agriculture, mining, and natural resources accounted for 50 percent of the gross national product, while manufacturing represented a little more than 5 percent, and the domestic saving rate was less than 7 percent (Congressional Budget Office 1997).

Government policy reforms in economics, education, and foreign aid transformed the South Korean economy so that by 2015 the GDP per capita was US$27,221.50, which was higher than that of Spain (US$25,831.60) (World Bank 2016). South Korea's GDP increased from US$8.9 billion in 1970 to a high of US$1.3 trillion by 2013, making it the 11th largest economy in the world according to the World Bank (as measured by GDP in U.S. dollars). South Korea's economy has grown by an average of 7 percent annually, with only two years over the last 50 years with contractions (Noland 2014).

This growth has been supported by an increase in exports, which accounted for only 2 percent of gross national product (GNP) in 1962, but nearly 32 percent in 1982. In 1954, South Korea exported to five countries, but by 1976 this number had increased to 175 countries (Congressional Budget Office 1997). As another indicator of the success of the Korean economic model, in 2010 South Korea transitioned from being an aid recipient to a donor when it became the newest member of the Organization of Economic Cooperation and Development (OECD) Development Assistance Committee (DAC).

GOVERNMENT POLICY AS A DRIVER IN SOUTH KOREA'S ECONOMIC SUCCESS

South Korea's economic success story has been traced to a variety of factors, including economic policies, development of conglomerates (*chaebols*) and weak small- and medium-sized firms, foreign aid, the demographic dividend that led to a large workforce, national education policies that resulted in a well-educated workforce, and strong social cohesion. I propose, however, that it was not merely any one factor, but rather the co-existence and interdependence of the chaebols and government policies that led to economic success, while the country benefited at the same time from positive demographic and social change. South Korea's rise from a low-income country to a major industrialized economy resulted from the mutual existence of all of these factors operating in tandem at an advantageous historical moment in the region.

Economic success began with military dictator (then president) Park Chung-hee's policy reforms in the 1960s that opened up the country to international trade and encouraged personal savings. The centralized government of Park's predecessor, President Syngman Rhee (1948–1960), was characterized as corrupt and lacking any economic vision, which resulted in a slow-growing economy in the 1950s because of few investments in industries and infrastructure. The lack of economic policy also resulted in South Korea's dependence on international aid, at the same time the country needed to rebuild its infrastructure following civil war. Aid from the United States and United Nations constituted a third of South Korea's total budget in 1954, peaked at 58.4 percent in 1956, and was approximately 38 percent in 1960. Aid from the United States was US$365 million in 1956 and was maintained at approximately US$200 million annually until the mid-1960s (U.S. Library of Congress n.d.). Breen (2010) sums up Rhee's time in office: "The best we can say about Rhee's 12 years in power was that his republic survived." Although Rhee technically resigned from office on April 26, 1960, he was forced out of office after student protests following a fraudulent presidential election in 1960 and general dissatisfaction with his repressive government.

In contrast, Park Chung-hee's authoritarian governance model had strong economic policies that reformed interest rates, imposed tighter fiscal policies, lowered trade barriers, and devalued the currency. This model was aided by a rapidly urbanizing labor force that benefited from an already strong education system (Congressional Budget Office 1997). Virtually no opposition to the policy changes was voiced, and the strong centralized government minimized the threat of organized labor movements.

South Korea's export-based economy benefited from a number of factors. Government policies favored exporters, especially in sectors such as chemical, iron, steel, and electronics, with shipbuilding exceptionally competitive. Also, regional integration with Japanese companies gave South Korea access to international markets, such as the United States and the European Economic Community/ European Union. "In 1972 nearly three-quarters of all Korean exports went to Japan and the United States, while 81 percent of imports to Korea came from those two countries" (Iwulska 2012, 63). In the following years South Korea diversified its target markets, which also allowed it to ride out the 2008 market downturn. "In 2009, 23 percent of total exports went to China, followed by the EU27 (12.8 percent), the United States (10.4 percent), and Japan (6.0 percent)" (ibid.). In addition, South Korea's membership in international associations such as Association of Southeast Asian Nations (ASEAN) and OECD fostered exports, as did the free trade agreements (FTAs) it entered into with countries such as Chile, India, and Singapore. While there is disagreement about the degree to which government policy positively affected the export economy, there is no disagreement that the chaebols were an integral part of the economic growth of the country.

CHAEBOLS

Chaebols are a conglomerate of major industrial companies concentrated around one holding company. The vertically integrated business groups usually hold shares in each other and are often run by one family. Examples include Samsung, LG, and Hyundai. As an example of the family connectivity, half the managers of various Samsung firms worked directly for the company's founder or his son in the "chairman's secretariat," and thus owed their allegiance to their patron(s) ("What Do You Do" 2011). Shares in the vast empires pass from one generation to the next using elaborate, byzantine ownership structures (Koo 2015). Kuk found that "38 percent of founders' sons had already inherited the founders' positions and 46 percent were in the positions to be group chairman sooner or later when their fathers retired" (1988, 128).

Starting in the 1960s, South Korea's rapid economic growth was influenced greatly by state interventionist policies that favored certain conglomerates through trade preference and other preferential rights (Noland 2014). Sectors that focused on foreign markets were granted special finance and tax policies by the government, including subsidizing transport costs and were allowed to import inputs at world prices (Iwulska 2012). The economic success has been stunning; South Korea's GDP in 2009 was more than 30 times higher than in 1960 (ibid.).

It has been argued that the chaebol system was as responsible for South Korea's economic success as nimble government policy, which capitalized on regional development in Japan and then China, as well as non-distorted labor costs. Conglomerates such as Hyundai and Samsung developed strong business empires as a result of the export-based development model. In turn, selected businesses received generous government-based loans and contracts, while wages were kept low. Sales from the 10 largest chaebols accounted for 80 percent of the country's GDP in 2011 (Koo 2015).

The Korean public may detest the chaebol system, but it remains powerful, and young people still vie for competitive job openings in firms such as Samsung. For some people chaebols are encompassing of life: workers may live in chaebol-owned apartments; shop at the chaebol-run department store; and watch popular TV soap operas that feature chaebols.

Although chaebols may be the ultimate job choice for many young adults, the system has been prone to corruption, fraud, and irregular accounting. Lee (1998) argued that the government and chaebols have a strategic alliance: politicians need campaign funds, and chaebols need capital for expansion. The rise and/or fall of each chaebol in the 1960s was still primarily a matter of political connections. During the Park Chung-hee administration the government intervened in the activities of chaebols directly through project management, allocation of foreign capital, and monopolization of financial institutions. The government attempted to reduce risk for selected chaebols by decreasing competition within the country, which led to their increased government dependence throughout the 1960s. The monopolization of products allowed chaebols to accumulate capital under government protection.

In addition, it is argued that chaebols stifle innovation and entrepreneurship ("What Do You Do" 2011). Chaebol empires may extend vertically from manufacturing and construction to retail and also build vertically by incorporating all stages of production into the empire. A few innovative Korean firms have prospered along with chaebols, but they tend to be the exception rather than the rule. The *Economist* ("Corporate Armistice" 2013) gave an example of Vinyl:

> a hip branding and technology company with about 200 employees, most of them under 40, some of whom wear shorts and decorate their desk with Iron Man action figures. Perhaps its greatest aspiration is that one day people will stop asking why it is called Vinyl. Its signature product is "Trans-

look", a transparent liquid-crystal display that can serve both as a window for displaying products and as a video screen for advertising them.

FOREIGN AID

Through the early 1960s, aid from the United States continued to be a critical component of South Korea's economic growth and success. Between 1953 and 1962, U.S. aid financed an average of 69 percent of South Korea's imports, making the country almost entirely dependent on the United States for food and consumer goods in the early postwar recovery years (USAID 2011). The USAID (and its predecessor the United States Operating Mission) provided a total of $18.7 billion (in constant 2009 U.S. dollars) in aid between 1952 and 1980 (ibid.). In the 1950s and 1960s, aid included large flows of military and economic support, substantial technical assistance, and the professional training in the United States of over 3,000 Koreans. The United States also aided infrastructure projects—such as electric, rail, and ports—that were critical to South Korea's development as a major exporter.

The South Korean government embraced development with intensity and developed the Economic Planning Board (EPB) as the primary unit for all development planning. During his tenure, Park Chung-hee visited the board at least monthly to review economic progress to date. USAID (and its predecessor) had a large advisory role in the board; USAID advisers worked alongside Koreans in the EPB and the Ministry of Finance. Dr. Joel Bernstein, a Chicago School economist and Korean mission director from 1964 to 1967, provided private economic consultations to President Park and his staff. Although Korean officials sought and received advice from the United States, South Korea made decisions independently of the advisers so its ministries could maintain their vision of development (USAID 2011).

U.S. advisers who served during the 1960s and 1970s recall the drive and focus of the South Koreans. USAID observed that Christopher Crowley, who served in USAID's Korea mission from 1976 to 1978, was struck by the pace of development: "They made up their mind and they did it. You'd go home one night, and there would be construction overnight, and the next morning a new building would be standing" (2011, 2). Marcus Winter, who served in the USAID Agricultural Planning Office in South Korea, also related that when demand for storage space (for fertilizer in the spring and rice in the autumn) was relayed to President Park Chung-hee during a visit to an agricultural area, the president declared, "Storage is a problem. We have got to solve this problem" (ibid.). Suddenly 320 warehouses were scheduled to be built in the joint U.S.-Korean agricultural program, and all warehouses were completed in 12 months, rather than the originally scheduled 18 months.

In the critical early years of development foundation building—between 1953 and 1963—the United States was the primary foreign aid donor, but starting in the mid-1960s, other organizations and countries stepped in. For example, the World Bank became a major multilateral donor to South Korea in 1962. Japan, the former occupier, became a donor in 1965 primarily through war reparations, and the Asian Development Bank began lending to South Korea in 1968. Foreign aid extended to rural areas as well: "AID, the Asian Development Bank, the World Bank, and the United Nations supported a massive irrigation effort between the early 1960s and the late 1970s. The results were positive, despite some cost overruns. Irrigated land increased from 662,000 hectares to 1,122,000" (Congressional Budget Office 1997, 19).

U.S. military assistance was also a critical transfer to South Korea and one that continues to this day. In terms of direct financial assistance, the

> U.S. military assistance to South Korea between 1953 and 1960—approximately $8.7 billion in 1997 dollars—aided South Korea's development in at least two ways. First, U.S. assistance helped build up the strong military establishment that South Korea needed to ensure its defense after the Korean War. By providing support for the defense budget, the United States allowed South Korea to devote resources to other, more productive sectors. (Congressional Budget Office 1997, 23)

In addition, the United States trained military officers and skilled laborers such as mechanics and electricians. In South Korea, serving as a military officer—then as now—became a major means of social mobility when officers transitioned into the labor force as leaders in conglomerates and the government.

The role of foreign assistance in the form of domestic and foreign savings can be seen in Table 2.1. As shown, the foreign transfers declined from 82.3 percent in 1960 to 4.3 percent in 1974, while at the same time total investment as a percentage of GNP increased

Table 2.1. Domestic and foreign saving (as a percentage of total investment), South Korea, 1958–1974

Year	Total investment as a percentage of GNP	DOMESTIC SAVING		FOREIGN SAVING	
		Private	Government	Transfers	Borrowing
1958	12.9	62.5	-24.1	69.8	-8.2
1959	10.7	61.5	-25.0	67.0	-3.5
1960	10.9	33.2	-18.7	82.3	-4.0
1961	13.1	42.8	-13.6	69.5	-4.3
1962	13.0	22.1	-10.7	72.9	10.0
1963	18.4	39.0	-1.4	37.8	20.6
1964	14.5	44.8	3.5	43.5	5.1
1965	14.7	38.1	11.5	44.2	-2.0
1966	21.6	41.6	13.0	26.5	12.5
1967	21.9	35.5	18.5	21.7	18.5
1968	26.7	27.5	23.5	14.6	28.5
1969	29.8	38.0	20.8	11.4	25.5
1970	27.2	34.5	25.5	8.0	27.4
1971	25.6	33.3	23.6	7.4	36.6
1972	20.9	53.1	18.6	8.3	18.4
1973	26.2	66.9	17.4	5.9	9.5
1974	31.4	51.7	9.6	4.3	38.9

GNP, gross national product.
Source: Congressional Budget Office (1997), based on data from Korean Economic Planning Board.

from 10.9 percent in 1960 to 31.4 percent in 1974. These parallel developments allowed South Korea to have a credit rating worthy of borrowing foreign capital in the 1960s and early 1970s, which was critical to the country's development because capital and natural resources were lacking. Although the percentages fluctuated (as seen in the far right column of Table 2.1), foreign borrowing was more than a third of total investments in 1971 and 1974.

Scholars have debated the role of foreign assistance in the 1960s and 1970s in South Korea's development. The United States started decreasing aid as early as the 1960s, but the timing coincided with President Park's economic reforms and the growth of human capital. It is evident, however, that the economic expansion would have been much slower without foreign assistance, and that South Korea would have been delayed in obtaining loans from other countries and organizations (Congressional Budget Office 1997).

THE DEMOGRAPHIC DIVIDEND AND THE LABOR FORCE

The South Korean labor force was also a major factor in the economic transformation. Not only was the labor force industrious and productive (described in the *Economist* ["What Do You Do" 2011] as being Stakhanovite), the ethnic and linguistic homogeneity of the country resulted in a lack of social segmentation and a high degree of equality. Land reform policies put into place after the Japanese occupation resulted in 90 percent of families owning land by 1953, an increase from 48 percent in 1945. The land redistribution diffused tensions and political instability, which were critical for labor force development. The economy also benefited from the relatively large cohorts of workers as a result of the demographic transition from a country with high fertility and high mortality to one with low fertility and low mortality. The numbers of workers increased steadily between 1970 and 2015. In percentage terms the working-age population increased from 54 percent of the total population in 1970 to 73 percent in 2015, or from 17 million to 37 million people in the same time period.

The first demographic dividend in South Korea commenced in 1971 when the support ratio (workers per consumers) began to increase from about two workers for every three consumers, to a high of 94 workers per 100 consumers from 2002 until 2012 when the ratio started to decline. The ratio will drop precipitously starting in about 2030. Lee and Mason (2013) estimate that between 1970 and 1999 the support ratio contributed 24 percent of the economic growth rate of 4.6 percent per annum. Between 2000 and 2050, however, they estimate that the effective labor force will grow more slowly than the effective numbers of consumers by approximately −0.45 percent per annum.

Several aspects of the South Korean labor force experience are notable. One is that Koreans have the highest labor force participation rates in the world for workers aged 65 and over, as discussed in more detail in Chapter 4. A comparison of labor force employment for males by five-year age group for Japan, South Korea, and United States are shown in Figure 2.1. Lee (2007) found that rural elderly

Figure 2.1.   Male labor force participation rates for Japan, South Korea, and the United States, 2015

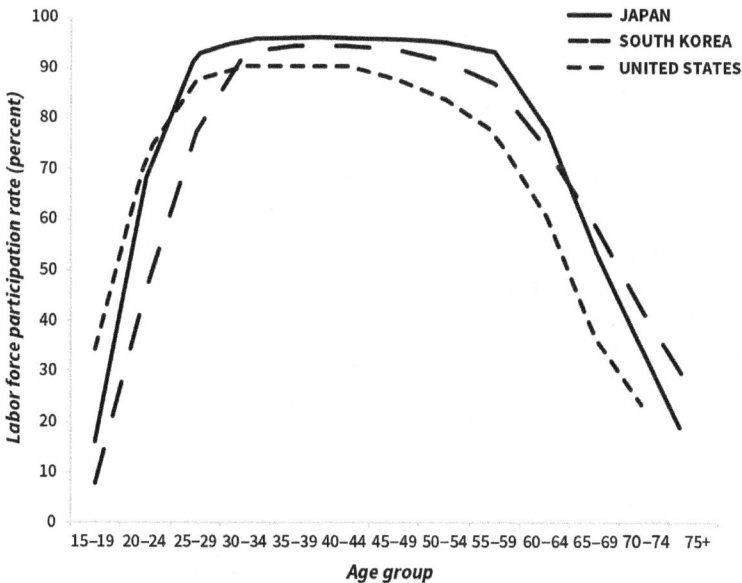

Source: OECD (2016b).

men were much more likely to be in the labor force than those in cities and surmised this could be a way to compensate for the absence of younger generations who might have migrated to urban areas. In other words, elderly men are working for an extended number of years in agriculturally based jobs because of lost family labor. Another possible explanation is that the current elderly are less likely to be covered by any social support program and might have had more difficulty accumulating savings, forcing them to continue working to avoid slipping even more behind financially.

THE EDUCATIONAL SYSTEM

In addition to the benefits provided by an industrious and hardworking labor force, South Koreans were and continue to be well educated. Investment in human capital through education as a means to economic growth and development was an especially wise decision by Park Chung-hee's administration considering South Korea's relative lack of natural resources. Crespo Cuaresma, Lutz, and Sanderson (2014, 300) have shown convincingly that improvements in education are a trigger for a fertility decline that in turn enhances economic growth. Rapid expansion of formal education occurred globally in the latter half of the twentieth century, but it was notable in South Korea because education outpaced economic growth. As a result, South Korea has reached higher levels of educational attainment than any other country at a similar level of economic development (Seth 2002). Education has driven the South Korean success story, and successive administrations have sought to coordinate education with state-directed economic goals in an attempt to maintain the country's economic momentum.

The Korean education system is both glorified and vilified at home and abroad (Ripley 2011). Sorensen (1994, 13) argued, "The educational success of present-day Korea ... has been brought about by an exceedingly complex interplay of values, institutions, economic resources, and accumulation of knowledge, and this interaction has taken place in a specific historical context of inter-

national economic and military relations and of national building."
As stated on the Ministry of Education's "Overview" web page
(2014), "Education in Korea has undergone numerous transformations and development through changing objectives according to
the needs of the times. The government set the direction for democratic education, expanding basic education to enhance democracy,
quantitative growth in education, education reform, and qualita-
tive growth of education." This direction has resulted in an extreme
preoccupation on examinations in a society that spends a greater
proportion of its income on education than any other country in
the world. To understand how the educational system developed
into its current form—and whether this is a benefit or a detriment
to the country—it is necessary to gain a historical understanding
of the system.

The Premodern Education System

Three important historical incidents influenced the modern Korean
educational system: (1) Confucianism, (2) American promotion of
equal opportunity in education, and (3) German schooling as im-
ported by the Japanese. In the year 372 (during the Goguryeo era),
Confucianism accompanied the earliest form of formal education
in Korea with the establishment of a form of higher learning
called Taehak, which consisted of training in morals, Confucianism, and Buddhism (Ministry of Education 2014). During the
Chosŏn period (also called the Joseon period: 1392–1910), education
was limited to the hereditary ruling class (*yangban*), which was estimated to be 15 percent of the population (Sorensen 1994). Confucianism stresses merit as the basis for judging individuals and
awarding status. In addition, Confucianism promotes every individual's potential to be a moral leader, with education as the vehicle
for moral perfection (Seth 2002).

The American influence was first felt when Christian missionaries started schools in the late nineteenth century and early twentieth century; by the time Japan annexed Korea in 1910, American

missionaries had established about 800 schools for 41,000 students (Kim 2003). The American system was later consequential in training the majority of university faculties following the end of Japanese occupation. Education in Korea is teacher- and textbook-centered with lectures and rote memorization the norm (Seth 2002), and Korean schools have never embraced American pedagogy. One lasting effect of the American influence, however, has been the ideal of universal and equal opportunity in education.

Education during the Japanese occupation (1910–1945) was restrictive for Koreans. The Educational Ordinance of 1911 set up a system with one educational track for Japanese residents and another for Koreans. The Japanese highly restricted mission schools, and the number declined from 823 in 1909 to 279 in 1920 (Seth 2002).

By 1942, approximately 40 percent of Korean children attended elementary school, but fewer than 5 percent went on to middle school, and accordingly, even fewer had the opportunity to enroll in high school (Sorensen 1994). Tertiary education was available only to a small percentage of the Korean population. Keijo Imperial University—later called Gyeongseong University, which became part of Seoul National University—was established in 1925 in Seoul and the majority of students were Japanese. Only 10 percent of Korean applicants were accepted to the University, in contrast with 40 percent of Japanese applicants, which created a source of resentment among the Korean elite (Seth 2002).

Several aspects of the early Korean and then Japanese educational systems have been carried over to modern times. The emphasis on rote memorization has survived from the early Korean system, as has the relationship between teachers and students. The Chosŏn education model facilitated the rise of examinations with a high degree of competition because passing those examinations accrued certain privileges (exemption from military duties) to the scholar (Seth 2002). In addition, the Japanese national system influenced a number of elements in the modern system, such as a high degree of centralization, an emphasis on elementary education, and later, development of secondary and tertiary education (ibid.). The colonial Japanese system featured enhanced state power and promoted a patriotic ideology that assimilated young Korean students to Japanese ultranationalism and militarization (ibid.).

The Seeds of the Modern Era of Education

South Korea, with assistance from the United States, started building a strong, centralized, and authoritarian state following liberation from Japanese rule in 1945. At the end of Japanese occupation, the illiteracy rate in South Korea was 78 percent (Sorensen 1994). The creation of an education system was critical, but faced a myriad of challenges. Neither the Koreans nor the Americans were prepared for Japan's collapse and had to react quickly with limited resources. One of the first acts of the new South Korean government was to establish the Ministry of Education in 1948, which controlled major aspects of education such as teacher certification, enrollments, and curricula.

Education also was a major focus of the newly formed Korean National Assembly. Although the Americans promoted the educational reforms of a progressive, democratic, decentralized education system during the United States' brief three-year occupation, South Korea retained an authoritarian, centralized school system. Korean educational leaders decided to maintain the status quo to accommodate the high demand for schooling. Furthermore, they were concerned the American system did not support the spiritual and moral content of the Korean schools that had been built on the Confucian traditions of the ethnically homogenous country (Seth 2002). A related decision concerned whether to adopt local school boards, as promoted by the United States, or to retain a centralized power structure. Although local school boards were authorized, and school associations were instituted to raise funds for schools, local school boards lacked power and were disbanded in 1961; parent associations were later revived in 1970 (ibid.).

A major point of discussion in developing an educational system was whether it should be more elitist as the Japanese system had been or more open and democratic like the American schools. In particular, this argument focused on whether the school system would provide a single track for all students or incorporate additional vocational schools. Proponents of the single-track system argued, "Korea required an educational system that would both produce qualified specialists with needed technical skills and ensure that the command posts of the new nation would be guided by only the brightest, most talented, and rigorously trained" (Seth 2002, 63). Others argued that while academic students needed three years of middle school and four years of high school to prepare for university studies, separate vocational schools would allow vocational training to start early for students who did not intend to continue on to high school or college. The supporters of vocational training believed that technical education was the key to building the flexible workforce needed to develop a modern economy.

In 1949, the National Assembly passed the Basic Education Law, Basic School Law, and Social Education Law, and voted in minor revisions over the next two years relating to the length and structure of middle and high schools. In 1951, the government decided to separate middle and high schools, with middle school lasting for three years as had been proposed by the Americans. This decision resulted in an "education ladder" of 6-3-3-4. In its current form, this ladder comprises six years of compulsory free education starting by age six; three years of free compulsory middle school; three years of noncompulsory high school; and four years of college. The Ministry of Education touts the ability of the single-track system to provide primary, secondary, and tertiary education for every child, according to the ability of the student, and without discrimination.

Although Korea rapidly expanded the educational system after Japanese occupation, development was problematic. One difficult task was recruiting teachers, particularly those who could teach in Korean. Before 1945, 40 percent of elementary teachers were Japanese, and many teachers educated during the Japanese occupation had been trained in Japanese (Seth 2002). Nearly all university professors were trained abroad. In addition, there was a demand for teachers to become administrators.

Korean textbooks were nonexistent and had to be developed in tandem with decisions made on the national curriculum; in some cases, textbooks from other countries were merely translated, even though the content was not always appropriate for Korea. Approximately 13 million textbooks were printed between September 1945 and February 1948 (Seth 2002).

Between 1945 and 1948, the percentage of children attending primary schools nearly doubled from less than 40 percent to 70 percent, and the number of secondary students increased six-fold (Seth 2002). Many of the newly built schools were destroyed during the Korean War (1950–1953), but a second boom in the number of students followed the war. One survey estimated that 80 percent of educational facilities were damaged or destroyed during the war and one-third of the schools were beyond repair (ibid.). The Korean War resulted in pent-up demand for schooling and enhanced the power of the South Korean state in all areas, including education (ibid.). The number of children in school continued to increase, even though many of the nation's schools had been destroyed in the war. Between 1955 and 1960, the number of primary school students rose from 2.9 to 3.7 million; middle school students from 475,000 to 529,000; and high school students from 142,000 to 164,000 (ibid.). Girls as well as boys enrolled, particularly in primary schools, making primary education nearly universal for all. The Korean people believed education was fundamental to economic development of the country, and nearly everyone saw education as the key to success. Slogans such as, "Don't be a farmer! Don't be a poor laborer!" infused the populace with a fervor for education (ibid.).

As a result, educational demand far outstripped supply, and the government inadvertently set up a system that would plague the country for years. For example, in 1953, entrance exams for middle and high schools were instituted so only the most qualified students would receive the highly sought-after secondary education. The middle school entrance exam was abolished in 1969, but by that point the country had already embraced an education mentality focused on examinations. This issue is addressed later in this chapter.

Educational Expansion

Once economic growth was under way in the early 1960s, efforts were made to increase the number of schools and enrolled students. Even with additional facilities and faculties, however, not enough qualified teachers could be found. Furthermore, teacher salaries remained low. The government started training teachers in earnest in the mid-1950s, providing in-service programs for teachers to advance their knowledge; hiring teachers with at least some college education also increased. Between 1952 and 1964, the percentage of primary school teachers with at least a two-year college degree increased from 1.6 to 15.8 percent (Seth 2002).

By 1966, educational demand had increased to such a point that a minimum of 28,000 additional classrooms were needed. Rapid urbanization, as well as the large number of children entering the school system for the first time, exacerbated already overcrowded classrooms. During the 1960s classes exceeded 80 students, and many primary schools ran two shifts, including some in Seoul that ran three shifts (Seth 2002). Schools simply could not keep up with the surging numbers of students enrolling at all levels; private schools at the secondary level provided one solution to the burden on public schools.

As seen in Figure 2.2, the number of primary students grew four-fold between 1945 and 1970 when primary school enrollment reached its apex. In the 1970s the number of young children started to decrease as a result of the fertility decline, a downward trend that has accelerated since 1980. Middle and high school enrollment reached their peaks in 1990 and have since declined, with the numbers roughly equal. The number of students in tertiary schools continued to increase and by 1995 had even surpassed the number of high school students, and now roughly equals the number of primary students. This trend of more tertiary students than high school students can be explained by several factors: (1) high school is only three years while college is four years, so it is expected there would be roughly 1.3 times as many college students as were in high school (if all high school students went on to college, and nearly

Figure 2.2.   Number of South Korean students enrolled in school by
level of school, 1945–2010

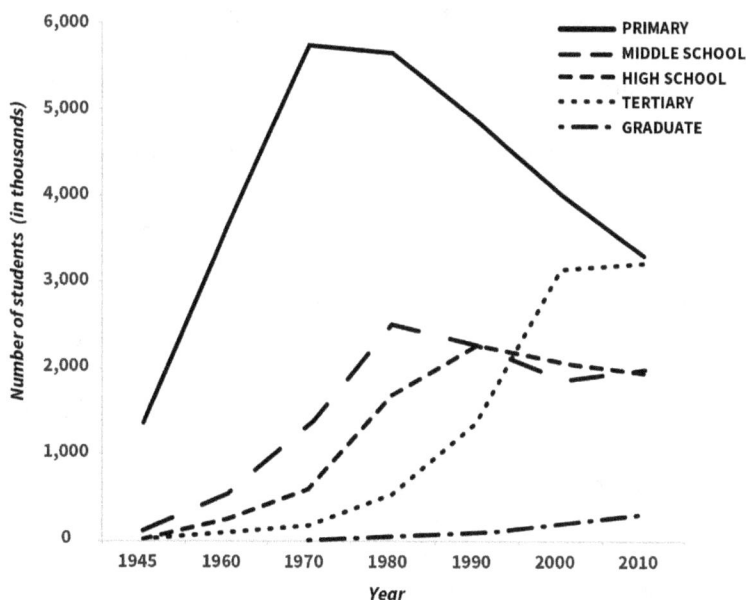

Sources: Ministry of Education (2014) and Shin (2011).

everyone does in South Korea); (2) slightly larger college-age cohorts
than younger cohorts; (3) the 54,540 international students (as of
2016) attending Korean schools (UNESCO 2017); and (4) Korean students who study outside of the country for high school, but return
for college. In 2006, 30,000 pre-college students left South Korea
solely to study abroad, but this number decreased to 18,000 in 2009
(Zagier 2012). These numbers do not include young people who accompanied their parents who work or study abroad. Many students
go to Canada, New Zealand, the United Kingdom, or the United
States to improve their English skills while they are relatively
young; as of 2009, 77 percent of the Korean pre-college students in
the United States were in primary or middle school (ibid.).

Although not shown in Figure 2.2, preschool and kindergarten
education also grew in popularity. As recently as 1980 only 901 kindergartens existed in the entire country, but as of 2017, South Korea

boasted 538,587 students attending 8,388 kindergartens (Ministry of Education 2017). The high rates of enrollment at all levels reflect the Korean government's strategic investment in an educated labor force over time. In 1955, the Ministry of Education received just under a tenth (9.3 percent) of the total government budget, but by 1985 that figure had grown to 19.9 percent (Jeong and Armer 1994). Various presidential administrations have emphasized different aspects of education to augment economic goals. For instance, to meet the demands of strategic industrial growth plans, the Park administration (1963–1979) emphasized secondary and technical education to produce educated, disciplined workers for the manufacturing sector, with only modest expansions at the tertiary level in technological, engineering, and science disciplines. This targeted expansion of secondary schools created a labor force primarily trained for factory work and industrial production (ibid.). At the time, strong control of educational resources allowed to the state to: (1) diminish barriers to entrance and (2) provide equal access to secondary schooling to boys and girls, students in urban and rural areas, and students of all economic classes, at least in theory.

A limited student quota intensified competition for middle schools, with enrollment peaking in the early 1980s. In 1971, the government expanded middle school quotas following its 1969 elimination of middle school entrance exams. Growth in middle school enrollment shifted pressure and competition, pushing it up the chain to high school admissions, particularly for highly regarded schools. In 1974, the government adopted a high school zoning policy that assigned students to schools in their residential district in an effort to mitigate competition among high school applicants in large and mid-sized cities. There were two noteworthy trends in the 1970s: (1) the quality of schools remained high and (2) enrollment gains were seen for females as well as males.

The increase in tertiary enrollment in the 1980s has largely been attributed to the movement of competition from high school to college and to major reforms adopted by the Chun Doo-hwan government, especially in relaxing college admission quotas (by 130 percent) in the 1980s and again in 1990 (Jeong and Armer 1994; Shin 2011). The rapid expansion in tertiary education has mostly relied on privately funded institutions operating independently of the government; South Korea leads the OECD countries with 80 percent of its students enrolled in private-sector institutions (Shin 2011). The growth of private universities allowed the government to allocate greater resources for elementary and secondary education, fueling interest in higher education nationwide. Comprehensive education reform policy established by the Kim Young-sam administration (1993–1998) was the catalyst for reform in higher education, both qualitatively and quantitatively. Kim's reforms shifted education toward knowledge production and development of national competitiveness in technology (ibid.).

As seen in Figure 2.3, the enrollment ratios (measured as number of enrollees ÷ number of graduates × 100) reached universality (at least 99 percent) for primary school by 1985 and for middle school

Figure 2.3. Enrollment ratios from one level of education to the next, South Korea, 1970–2005

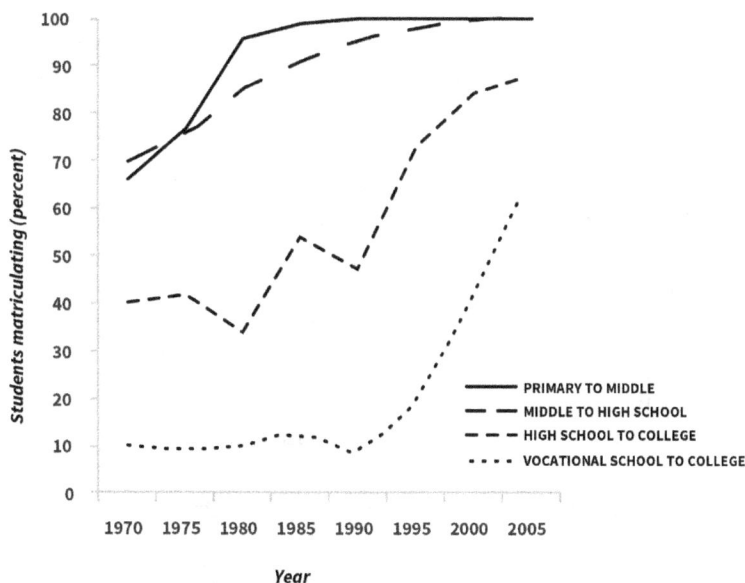

Source: Ministry of Education (2014).

by 1997. The rapid increase in the percentage of students from regular as well as technical high schools attending college is notable. Ninety-seven percent of 18-year-olds graduate from high school (Kim 2008); in 2003, 90.2 percent of high school graduates started college, though the percentage has declined slightly since then. The percentage of students from technical high schools starting college has continued to increase as well, with 71.5 percent attending college in 2007, the most recent date for available data.

The demand for college is so high that a sizeable number of Korean students study abroad; in fact, after China, India, and Germany, South Koreans make up the fourth largest absolute number of students studying abroad (UNESCO 2017). In 2016, for example, 108,047 Korean students studied abroad, with approximately 60 percent attending U.S. schools. It is estimated that Koreans studying abroad (at all levels) spent US$4.6 billion on tuition and living expenses in 2006 (Kim 2008). A large percentage of Koreans study abroad for advanced degrees. For instance, more than 9 out of 10 (93 percent) of faculty members at Korea's Pohang University of Science and Technology received a Ph.D. in the United States; at Yonsei, Seogang, and Ewha Universities 4 out of 5 faculty members received a U.S.-based Ph.D. (ibid.).

As described earlier, the growth of higher education in South Korea has been marked by its quality as well as quantity. Korean higher education has been successful largely because of the government's development of the critical building blocks of elementary, middle, and high schools; the system should continue to be effective in the government's pursuit of a knowledge-based economy. One area of tremendous growth has been junior colleges. Originally, terminal degrees were considered only for vocational training, but starting in the 1980s, firms began hiring junior college graduates; by 1991, 87 percent of junior college graduates were placed in an appropriate job for their educational level (Seth 2002). This phenomenon may be in part due to what the Ministry of Education (2014) calls "a practical curriculum through on-site training via school-industry cooperative programs, vocational specialty training plans and job sheets. Specialization is stressed as preparation for the National Certification Examination. Work ethics are also instilled." In 1970, 33,483 students attended junior college; the most recent number is 767,087 (Ministry of Education 2017).

SOCIAL COHESION

As mentioned earlier, as Korea emerged from its physical devastation in the 1950s one aspect that helped the country develop its social and economic strength was social cohesion. Korea has a national mythology of being a homogenous and united country or unitary race (*danil minjok gukka*) (Hundt 2016).

Adelman (2014, 12) proposes social capital, which includes "not only the level of human resources but also the degree of social cohesion, the willingness to act for the social good, and the extent of social trust, cooperative norms and the density of interpersonal networks" generated economic development. Even with rapid economic growth in the 1960s and 1970s, the benefits of economic growth appear to have been shared more equitably across economic classes in Korea than in other developing countries. As one measure of income inequality, the Gini index defines the index gap between rich and poor in a country and ranges between 0 and 1, with 0 representing perfect equality and 1 representing perfect inequality. The Gini index in South Korea was 0.344 in 1965, 0.332 in 1970, and 0.302 in 2014. In comparison, in 2013, the Gini index was 0.529 for Brazil, 0.481 for Bolivia, and 0.517 for Panama (World Bank 2016).

The decrease in the Gini coefficient, however, is misleading when looking at South Korea. The beneficial effects of the country's economic miracle have not been felt equally by all age cohorts, particularly the elderly populations, as discussed at length in Chapter 4. To gain a more nuanced understanding of whether development has promoted or slowed social cohesion it is critical to understand the first—and potentially second—demographic dividend in South Korea.

SUMMARY

As described in this chapter, the East Asian miracle of economic growth was accompanied by the precipitous decline in South Korean fertility starting in the 1970s as well as agrarian reform, rapid urbanization, expanded schooling, and authoritarian government policies, all of which strengthened the export-based economy. These factors resulted in a relatively large working-age population situated at the crossroads of economic expansion.

The highly touted economic miracle in South Korea in the second half of the twentieth century was brought about by an interlocking set of factors: government policies favoring an export economy, development of the chaebol system, infusion of foreign aid, the demographic dividend, the education dividend, and strong social cohesion. The combination of these led to social changes that will be described in more detail in the following chapters. While South Korea's economic growth has been astounding, it is misleading to focus only on the economy.

The following two chapters detail the divergence between the working-age population and the elderly in reaping the benefits of the first demographic dividend. Although it can be argued that South Korea as a whole benefited from the education dividend, as discussed in this chapter, and economically from the demographic dividend, some subgroups—the rural population, elderly, and women—have benefited far less or not at all from the demographic dividend in terms of quality of life. Chapters 3 and 4 examine the generational schism of the demographic dividend in relation to cultural changes, particularly the movement away from Confucian traditions in South Korea.

3. SOCIAL CHANGE IN THE MIDST OF ECONOMIC GROWTH

Economically, the working-age population has benefited from the demographic dividend. The South Korean gross domestic product (GDP) increased from US$8.9 billion in 1970 to a high of US$1.4 trillion in 2014 (see Figure 3.1). Real GDP per capita increased from US$1,537 in 1960 to an estimated US$35,853 in 2016 (OECD 2017b; Shin and Park 2013). This chapter examines the benefits of the economic transformation for those in the current working ages and highlights the societal costs of the transformation to the industrialized South Korea of the twenty-first century. The economy suffered greatly in 1997, but reforms put in place following the International Monetary Fund crisis allowed the country to rebound easier and more quickly when the 2008 global crisis occurred.

URBANIZATION

We start the analysis for this chapter by examining the spatial and familial changes that have altered the most basic aspect of life: where people live and with whom. Urbanization came to South Korea at a rapid rate, from 40 percent in 1970 to 83 percent by 2012, which has leveled off since that time. Seoul has long been established as the capital of Korea, dating back to 1394 and the Chosŏn Dynasty. In 2015, Seoul's population was 9,904,312 and contained approximately 25 percent of the country's urban populace. Although the population density for the entire country in 2015 was 509 persons per square kilometer (316 people per square mile), the population density for Seoul was 16,364 people per square kilometer (10,168

Figure 3.1.   Gross domestic product (in current U.S. dollars),
South Korea, 1970–2016

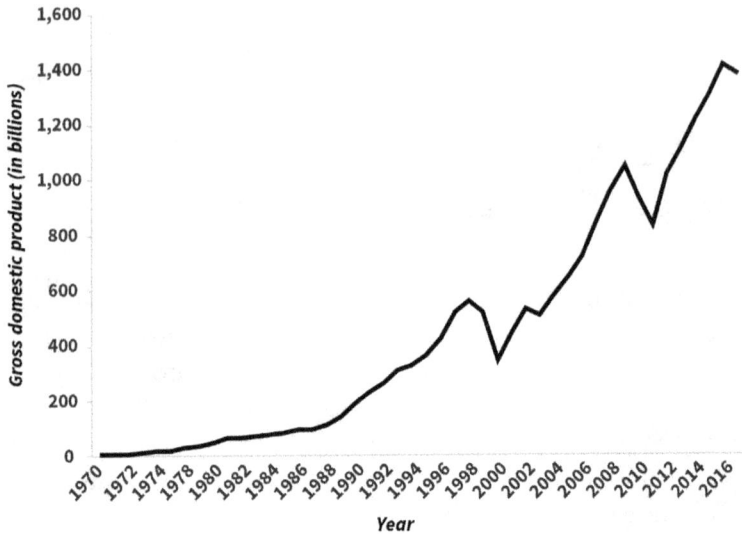

Source: World Bank (2017).

persons per square mile) (KOSIS 2017), in comparison to Singapore
at 10,200 persons per square kilometer (Brodie 2017).

To put South Korea's rapid urbanization in perspective, it took
the United States 100 years (1790–1890) for the urban population to
grow from 5 percent to 35 percent and 220 years (1790–2010) for
it to reach 81 percent (U.S. Census Bureau 2015). Japan is more
urban, but its growth in the last 65 years was also slower than South
Korea's. Japan's urban population was 50 percent in 1950, which increased to 79 percent by 2000 and by 2014 stood at 92 percent.
China has been slower to urbanize: 13 percent in 1950, 36 percent in
2000, and 53 percent in 2014 (United Nations 2002; World Bank
2015).

As with most aspects of South Korea, the federal government has
played a major role in how urbanization has taken place, creating a

complex administrative structure for provinces and cities.* Starting in 1988 the government unveiled a five-year housing plan, the Two Million Home Construction Plan, to tackle severe shortages in housing and soaring housing prices by adding housing units around Seoul in five new cities: Bundang, Ilsan, Jungdong, Sanbon, and Pyeongchon. Individuals and businesses received tax benefits as an incentive to move to the new towns. With the increase in housing prices in Seoul, another set of new cities were developed near Seoul: Pangyo, Dongtan, Uijeongbu, and Gimpo. These new cities have been designed to alleviate the overpopulation problem and ensure residential stability in the Seoul Metropolitan Area. The plan for these cities called for construction from 2001 to 2015 to accommodate 1.53 million people (Lee 2012). The most recent addition is Sejong City, located 120 kilometers (75 miles) from Seoul, whose population increased from 875 in 2011 to 204,088 in 2015 (KOSIS 2017). Plans for the new city include a total population of 500,000 by 2030, with an urban area of 465 square kilometers (179.6 square miles). When complete the city will house 36 government organizations with as many as 13,000 civil servants (Harlan 2012). One reason for the development of Sejong City was for security reasons as it is further away from the border with North Korea (BBC 2012).

South Korea's urbanization was made possible through its parallel change in economic structure from an agrarian to an industrial economy in a short time. In 1960, for example, the agricultural sector contained 80 percent of the labor force (Choe and Kim 2001). By 1980, agricultural employment had decreased to 34 percent in 1980, and by 2010 it was only 7 percent (World Bank 2015). The

---

* Seoul is classified as a special city; Busan, Daegu, Incehon, Gwangju, Daejon, and Ulsan are classified as metropolitan cities; and Sejong is a special autonomous city. Cities in South Korea have a population of at least 150,000; once a county (*gun*) reaches that size, it becomes a city (with the exception of Gijang County in Busan). Most cities with more than 500,000 persons are further divided into districts and neighborhoods. The government developed a "new city" policy in the 1960s that led to the development of Ulsan in 1962 and Phang in 1968 as industrial cities. Gumi was added in 1973 and Changwon and Yeocheon in 1977 for expansion of exports and to develop and promote chemical industries.

switchover to the urban, industrial labor force was facilitated by a relatively cheap, but well-educated, labor force. Rapid urbanization has been one of the greatest transformations in South Korea in the past century, resulting in both negative and positive consequences. On the plus side, the massive urbanization and growth of the industrial sector was largely driven by the export market, which gave South Korea a prominent position in the global market. On the negative side, urbanization has been marked by extensive growth beyond administrative boundaries. Metropolitan governance has been weak in general, so even within cities there is a need for policies to address improved infrastructure and urban environments (Choe and Kim 2001).

LIVING SPACES

Not only has urbanization changed where people live, but it also has dramatically changed how people live and with whom, which has changed family structure and intensified or continued gender stratification. As of 2006 nearly four-fifths of Koreans owned their homes, with only 21 percent living in rented housing units, many of which had long-term leases (Park 2009).

As seen in Figure 3.2, in 1980, 90 percent of Koreans lived in detached dwellings, which decreased to 40 percent in 2010. Conversely, the percentage of apartment households increased from 5 percent in 1980 to 48 percent by 2010. This trend toward apartment living parallels the trend of urbanization; according to Park (2009), all ages seek apartment living because of its amenities, including a modern kitchen, easy maintenance, heating, and air conditioning.

The rise in housing construction has been key to South Korea's booming economy. Between 1962 and 2007, about 15 million new homes were built, of which 10.8 million were built between 1989 and 2007 (Ronald and Lee 2012). This building boom has in large part alleviated chronic housing shortages that had plagued the country, especially in Seoul, until the mid-1990s. This construction pace is remarkable considering the 2010 census counted 17.3 million households in the entire country. In essence, the housing stock for

Figure 3.2. Percentage of South Koreans living in detached dwellings, apartments, and all other types of housing, 1980–2010

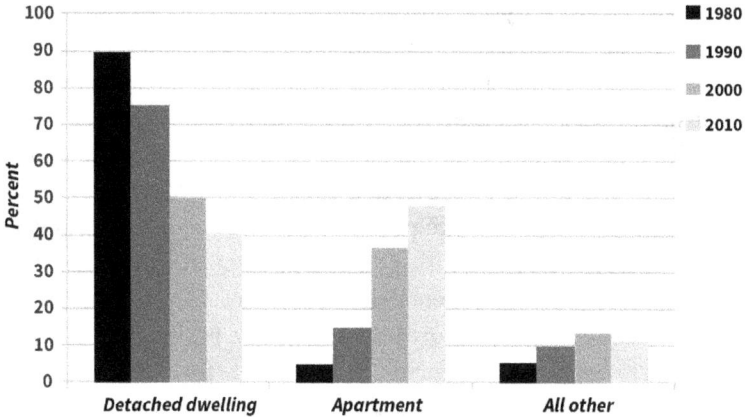

Source: KOSIS (2015).

the entire country has been built in the last 50 years, and nearly two-thirds in the past 25 years.

The downside of the rise in construction is that housing prices and utility costs have crept upward since 1985, as evidenced by results from the monthly Consumer Price Survey produced by the Korean Statistical Information System (KOSIS). The survey reports monthly costs for housing, water, electricity, and other fuels. To compute a yearly figure, the 12-month figures were averaged, with 2010 used as the index year. The Korean housing consumer price index was 37 in 1985 and rose steadily to 116 in 2014. Subsidized rental housing for low-income families began in 1971 with about 5,000 to 7,000 units built each year in the 1970s. Since then a variety of government programs have been initiated with the intent of helping household heads to become homeowners (Ronald and Lee 2012).

Another trend in how the Korean people live has been the move toward smaller households. In 1980, less than 5 percent of the population lived in one-person households; by 2010, that number had increased to nearly 24 percent. Conversely, 50 percent of households in 1980 contained five or more persons, whereas only 8 percent did so in 2010 (KOSIS 2015). The change in household composition is accounted for by a movement toward nuclear families, delay in marriage, popularity of living alone, and smaller family sizes, which will be discussed in more detail later in this chapter. The rapidity with which South Korea experienced the change in household size brings into question the prevalence of living alone. In a detailed analysis, Park and Choi (2015) reported that in 1980 about 1 percent of men aged 25–34 lived alone; by 2010 this number had increased to 15 percent. The pattern was even more pronounced for never-married men with over 20 percent of never-married men aged 25–34 living alone. Although increases for women in the same age group were noted over the same period (from about 1 percent to 10 percent), the primary change was for elderly women, which will be discussed in more detail in Chapter 4. Also of interest in Park and Choi's study was that young adults, particularly women, with less than a tertiary education were more likely to live alone than their counterparts. This may be indicative of young adults from more affluent families staying longer in the parental home until they are ready to marry and establish a home with a spouse. I conclude the reasons for the Korean population's shift to living alone are part of the interwoven social changes that have accompanied rapid urbanization, expansion of the educational system, and the shift away from Confucian values.

RETREAT FROM MARRIAGE

As discussed earlier, South Korea's rapid transition to a highly urban population as a part of the demographic dividend affected the entire country, and the transition has had a powerful effect on family structure. In addition, the arrangement and function of South Korean familial relationships are affected strongly by persistent gender inequalities in the labor market, highly segmented gender division between formal labor and domestic work for women, and strong social norms. This section examines South Korea's movement from stem to nuclear families and the results of changes in family structure on everything from a loss of intergenerational relationships to low fertility.

A clear retreat from marriage in South Korea exists as a result of the Asian version of the second demographic transition (SDT), as discussed in Chapter 1. The declining marriage rate is primarily a result of the prolonged number of years spent in school and delayed entry into the labor force. As a result, more people are remaining single, and concurrently the divorce rate has increased over time. These marriage trends have major implications for Korean society, the economy, and even politics, though South Korea is not alone in this trend. Most East Asian countries are experiencing the same pattern of delayed marriage or no marriage. The mean age at marriage in Japan, Taiwan, and Hong Kong, for example, is between ages 31 and 33 for men, and between ages 29 and 30 for women. As of 2010, 37 percent of Taiwanese women aged 30–34 were single ("The Flight from Marriage" 2011). In Japan during the early 1970s more than a million couples married each year; in 2013, only 661,000 marriages occurred; and almost half (49.1 percent) of women aged 25–34 in 2010 had never married (Jones 2007; Statistics Japan 2015).

In South Korea the number of marriages reached an apex in 2011 with 399,087 couples marrying. The number had increased between 1970 (295,137 couples) and 2011, and has since declined with an estimated number of 281,635 marriages in 2016. The marriage rate (marriages per 1,000 persons) declined from its apex in 1980 of 10.6 to 5.5 in 2016. As seen in Figure 3.3, the marriage rate has fluctuated over time, whereas the divorce rate increased up until the last few years and has since leveled off. Another way of measuring the change in marriage structure is the ratio of marriages per divorce in a given year (KOSIS 2016). In 1970, 25.4 marriages occurred for every divorce in that year, and in 2016 the ratio was 2.6 marriages for every divorce.

The mean age at marriage in South Korea is similar to its neighbors; as of 2010 the mean ages for women and men, respectively, were 28.9 and 31.8 years ("Koreans Marry Later than Ever" 2011). This shows an increase from 1960 when the mean age for women

Figure 3.3.   Marriage and divorce rates, South Korea, 1970–2016

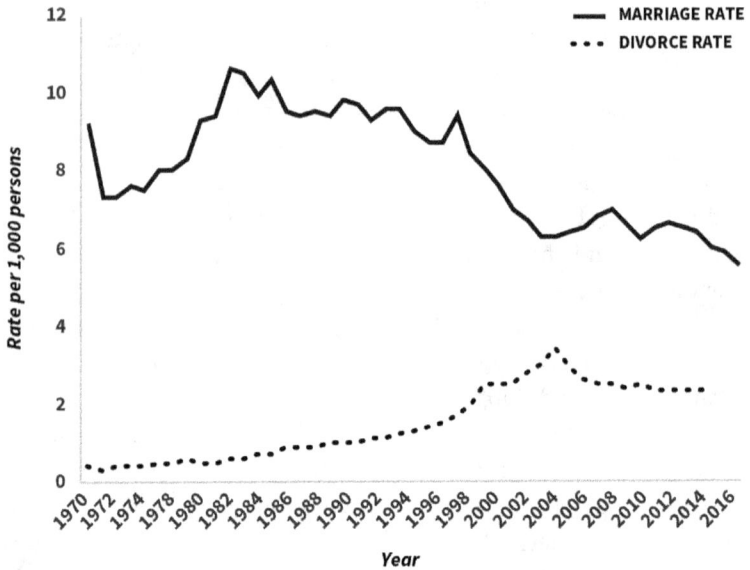

Source: KOSIS, Vital Statistics (2016).

was 21.5 years and 25.3 years for men (Choe 2006). The age difference at time of marriage has narrowed over time from 3.8 years in
1960 to 2.9 years in 2010.

In South Korea, generational differences in the importance of
marriage are evident; in a recent survey conducted by the government, only 9 percent of persons aged 20–39 reported marriage was
imperative, while 34 percent of those aged 60–69 believe it is (Denney
2015). Traditionally, matchmakers and family connections assisted
in finding marriage partners. As more families moved away from
ancestral homes, dating services became more common, but meeting
someone online has not met with the success it has in countries such
as the United States. With the decline in marriage, however, the
government has moved into the matchmaking role. In a cleverly
titled "Mom Wants You Married? So Does the State," the *New York
Times* reported that the Korean Ministry of Health and Welfare
held four dating parties in 2010, and since then ministry affiliates

and local governments have sponsored dating parties (Lee 2013). One couple who met at a government-sponsored party was featured in a magazine article, but the overall success of the parties in assisting young people find marriage partners remains unknown. Results of changes in Korean family structures, including the retreat from marriage, appear to have different roots for various socioeconomic groups. For instance, delayed and foregone marriage has followed the rise in female educational levels and female labor force participation. As a result, women with the highest levels of education and high-paying jobs most keenly feel the marriage squeeze if traditional norms of "marrying up" (or hypergamy) are in place. It may not only be that highly educated women find the pool of marriageable men limited, but it is difficult to find men that share the same values toward gender roles. In addition, women with a great deal of workplace autonomy may be less interested in childrearing, which would limit their working hours and could result in leaving the job: either short-term or permanently. Also, a highly educated woman may not want to take on traditional intergenerational responsibilities of caring for her husband's elderly parents along with her own. South Korea traditionally has had a history of heterogamy (Park and Smits 2005), but as educational differences have narrowed between men and women (educational) homogamy has become more common among those who do marry, while at the same time educational homogamy has been one factor leading to a decline in marriage rates.

For men, particularly highly educated men, a highly educated partner may be ideal if she can help their children succeed in the highly competitive educational system (described in Chapter 2). This situation puts women with low educational levels at an extreme disadvantage in the marriage market. Park, Lee, and Jo (2013) found that of women born between 1971 and 1980 who had had not graduated from high school, nearly 20 percent had never married by the age of 39; the authors hypothesized that the majority of those unmarried by age 40 would never marry.

Thus, the overall trend in South Korea is toward later and fewer marriages, especially compared with previous generations;

delayed marriage is most evident among women with the most and least education, but for varying reasons. Interestingly, in addition to the societal/normative reasons to postpone or forego marriage, the high cost of a Korean wedding, which Reuters reports may cost as much as US$200,000, can be a deterrent. This figure may be slightly misleading as much of the wedding cost goes toward securing housing, which continues to stretch budgets. As Shin (2012) reported, the rapid rise in wedding costs far outstrips regular inflation, which increased by 270 percent between 1999 and 2011. As well as an investment in a home, wedding expenses include gifts between the families and hosting hundreds of guests, many of who may only know parents of the bride or groom; however, the wedding guest list itself represents the status of the family. In a recent survey, 76 percent of Koreans aged 13 and over reported that wedding expenses and procedures were excessive (Statistics Korea 2014).

MULTICULTURAL MARRIAGES

Structural economic and social inequality paired with regional differentiation means men from the poorest and most rural regions of South Korea find it most difficult to find marriage partners. Young people in rural settings face challenges in the marriage market because (1) so few people of marriageable age reside in rural areas and (2) young men are faced with finding brides willing to accept the agrarian, and often more traditional, lifestyle. Two commonly employed options have been for bachelors to co-reside with elderly parents in their rural home, which Chang (2013) refers to as a distorted stem familial structure, and, more recently, to marry a woman from another country. The number of multicultural marriages fluctuate yearly, but approximately 1 out of 10 marriages in South Korea includes an international spouse. Over the last 15 years, the number of Korean women marrying a foreign husband is about 20–25 percent of the total yearly interracial marriages, which means predominantly Korean men marry women from another country. Marked differences exist in the rates of international marriages between urban and rural areas, with as many as

1 out of 3 marriages in rural areas occurring with a bride from another country (ibid.). The *Economist* ("The Flight from Marriage" 2011) reports that 44 percent of South Korean men who married in 2009 took a foreign bride. Beginning in 1992, after China and South Korea established diplomatic relations thousands of Chinese women of Korean descent (Joseonjok)—mostly from impoverished families—immigrated to rural areas as brides. As that flow of women decreased, potential brides started arriving from Vietnam, China, and the Philippines. Banners advertising wedding halls and banquet services for Vietnamese brides could be seen throughout rural areas (Kim and Jaffe 2010, 221).

Marriage to a foreign bride has not been without problems. In South Korea, the term *damunhwa*, which literally means multiculture in English, is used in South Korea as an adjective meaning multicultural. For instance, a multicultural society is *damunhwasahoe* and multicultural families are *damunhwagajok*. Park and Stephen (2013) found in social media that native-born Korean "netizens" (Internet users) were concerned about government policies and the current reality of multiculturalism in the country.

Although Koreans are keenly aware of multiculturalism, currently no effective solution exists to soothe the turbulent discourse that multiculturalism is creating. Much angst penetrating the Internet in forms of inflammatory comments and radical cyber congregations is created by a multifaceted misunderstanding and swelling fears on the part of native-born Koreans. Without an effort to address such grievances, damunhwa issues may expand into a complicated form of ethnic conflict that may pose great challenges unprecedented in this homogenous country. As many as 40 percent of mixed-race marriages end within the first five years ("Farmed Out" 2014), and the Ministry of Gender Equality and Family (MoGEF), reported that 41.3 percent of multicultural families said that they had experienced discrimination in 2012 (Kang 2013). In an attempt to stem the tide of difficulties, the MoGEF has taken a proactive stance to provide pre-marriage education to international brides before they even arrive in South Korea. Centers exist in Vietnam, the Philippines, and Mongolia with new centers being built in Cambodia and Uzbekistan.

The government has opened 200 multicultural centers that offer language classes, interpreting, and counseling at a cost of about US$105 million; however, assimilation remains elusive and affects the entire family. Many mothers have limited Korean-language skills, and as many as one-fifth of school-age children from mixed-race households were not attending class ("Farmed Out" 2014). As recently as 2013, however, the MoGEF reported plans to add 1,400 assistants in elementary schools to assist multicultural children adjust academically. Hyunjoon Park (2007, 195) summarized the difficulties of assimilation and the educational system,

> Unless South Korean society as a whole questions its assumption of cultural homogeneity and is willing to embrace foreigners and immigrants, its education system will not be able to address effectively the educational disadvantages of children born in these families. Without social and cultural transformations, the emerging family types will become significant source of variations in South Korean children's educational outcomes.

DIVORCE AND REMARRIAGE

As was observed in Figure 3.3, divorce rates in South Korea increased between 1980 through the early 2010s, when the rates leveled off. The social and economic costs of a divorce, however, are particularly high for women given their difficulties in achieving economic independence and norms after divorce. The Asian marriage system incorporates a distinctive divorce pattern, at least in Japan and South Korea. Recent research on divorce in Japan has shown a negative relationship between divorce and education, although the reasons for this pattern remain elusive (Park and Raymo 2013). Using vital statistics records for South Korea for all divorces registered between 1991 and 2006, Park and Raymo detected patterns similar to that of Japan. Although divorce increased at all levels of education, it was more pronounced for women and men with a high school education or less. Because the authors were using vital records, limited demographic and socioeconomic data about the couples existed so they could not examine income or other variables that might be important correlates. Given the findings that women with the least education are less likely to marry than women with at least a high school education, and that divorce rates are highest for women with lower levels of education, strong family norms may be weakest among this group. Further research should attempt to distinguish among family systems of various socioeconomic/educational groups in South Korea with the realization there is no single Asian family-building model, or even one single Korean marriage model.

As a result of the increase in divorce and changing norms in South Korea, remarriage rates increased from 4.1 percent in 1980 (for women) to 14.5 percent in 2000 (Cho 2013). Family law has been slow to adjust in response to the societal changes in the country because of the *hoju* system, the patriarchal family registry system in which women were legally subject to the male head of the family. Upon marriage, a woman was transferred (or changed) from being her father's dependent to her husband's dependent. The husband's signature was required for all legal paperwork and all aspects of daily life. This system, which dates back to 1898, was abolished on January 1, 2008, and has been replaced with an individual registration system that gives more legal rights to remarried women, such as the possibility of children changing their family name with the court's approval.

GENDER INEQUALITY AND THE GENDERED LABOR MARKET

Gender inequality in South Korea is pervasive and remains prevalent in many aspects of life. Strong patriarchal values from the Confucian past still persist, even though women have made tremendous gains in education and labor force participation. Improvements in the social, political, and legal areas also have been slow and limited for South Korean women. In the family, strong gender roles persist and son preference remains deeply entrenched (Park and Cho 1995), which pervades all aspects of the social fabric of South Korea, including the labor market.

For years South Koreans lodged the most work per year of any other Organization for Economic Cooperation and Development (OECD) country; in 2008 Mexico surpassed South Korea for the first time and retained that position through 2016. Koreans are now working the second longest hours (OECD 2017a). As of 2016, Koreans worked an average of 2,069 hours per year (39.8 hours per week), compared with the OECD average of 1,763 hours per year (33.9 hours per week). The long hours create strain for working mothers and place more of a burden on women whose employed husbands spend limited time with their families.

The global financial crisis of 2007–2008 also affected the status of many Korean workers, particularly in the percentage of part-time and irregular workers. In 2005, only 9 percent of Koreans held part-time positions, but that percentage reached an apex of 13.5 percent in 2011, following successive increases in part-time work after the 2007–2008 financial crisis. As of 2014, the percentage of part-time workers had declined to 10.5 percent. Although rates increased for men and women, as of 2014 nearly two-thirds of part-time workers were women. The male labor force consisted of 93.2 percent full-time workers, but female full-time workers were only 84.4 percent of the workforce (OECD 2016b). Although the trend toward part-time/irregular work results in cost savings for companies, by allowing them to cut salaries and benefits, the short-term effects for individuals is lost or limited benefits and the long-term effects will reverberate for years with diminished pensions and/or personal savings.

Traditionally women in South Korea have been marginalized in the domestic and public spheres as a result of the hierarchical family structure supported by Confucianism and by successive authoritarian military regimes that maintained laws and policies. Although gender discrimination is outlawed, gender inequality in hiring, promotions, earnings, and retirement support continues. In the early 1990s, following the international movement of gender equality, this became a major social policy issue in South Korea, but it will take years to move past a history of gender segregation in the family and the workplace.

For instance, during the rapid expansion of the manufacturing sector the female employment rate increased faster than that of males. In the 1970s, female labor dominated export industries such as textiles, clothing, electronics, and footwear (Kong 2013). Young women were critical in transforming the economy, but received wages less than half of what men earned (Cho 2013). Gender segregation in the Korean labor force also reflects women's lack of power. The proportion of women in managerial positions was only 0.5 percent in 2008, an increase from 0.3 percent in 2000, but still indicative of female marginalization in the top ranks (Kong 2013). This lack of power also is reflected in the educational sector. As of 1998, 50 percent of primary through high school teachers were women, but women accounted for only 6 percent of assistant principals and 5 percent of principals (Seth 2002).

One issue affecting female participation in the labor market centers around women being viewed as temporary employees who work only until marriage. South Korean women traditionally join the labor market after completion of a tertiary degree, then retreat from the labor force during their 30s to have children, begin to rejoin the labor force in their 40s, and end labor force participation in their 50s, a tendency that accelerates in their 60s. This M-shaped pattern of women's participation can be seen in Figure 3.4. In 2015, female labor force participation in South Korea had two peaks: first for 25–29-year-old women, with a rate of 72.9 percent; then for 45–49-year-old women, with a rate of 70.4 percent. The M-shaped configuration is much more accentuated in South Korea than in Japan or the United States. As is evident in Figure 3.4, women in Japan show more of an n-shaped pattern with the peak employment in the 25–29 age group (80.3 percent), but less of a trough in the primary reproductive and early-mothering years as is the case in South Korea. The United States shows a lazy-C pattern in which women's employment levels rise through their 20s and remain relatively stable through their 30s and 40s, with the first declines coming in their 50s, which accelerates in their 60s. Not only do labor force patterns differ among the three countries, it is also evident that labor force participation for Korean women remains very low compared

Figure 3.4.   Female labor force participation rates by age group for
Japan, South Korea, and the United States, 2015

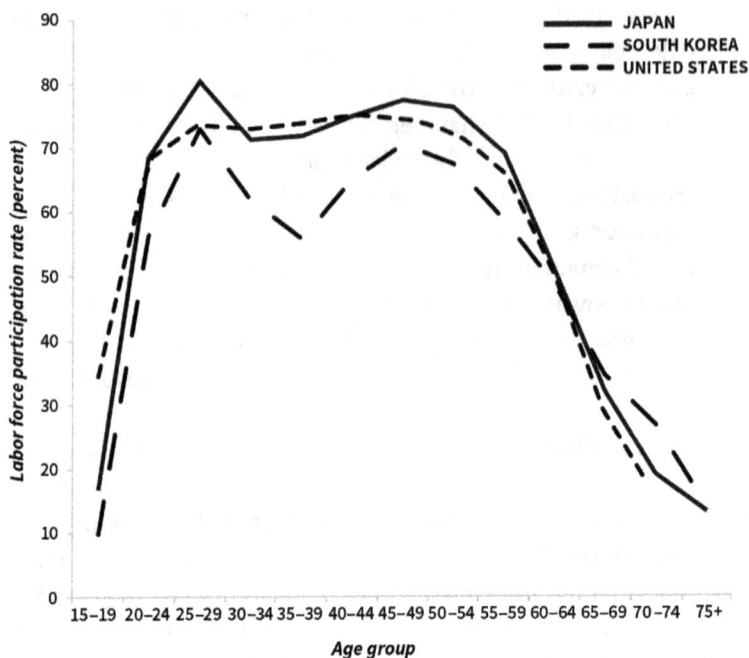

Source: OECD (2016a).

to women in other developed countries and among Asian countries.
In April 2017, for example, of the 22,267,000 Korean women aged 15
and over, 11,803,000 were employed, for a female labor force participation rate of 53 percent, compared with the male rate of 74 percent
(KOSIS 2017). During the 1997–1998 Asian financial crisis, women
were more likely to be fired than men; in the clerical sector, 1 out of
every 5 women lost her job between July 1998 and March 1999 while
only 1 out of 12 men did so (Cho 2013).

Although efforts have been made to eliminate gender discrimination in the Korean work place, researchers have found bias in job
entry, earnings, and promotion (Keong-Suk Park 2007). The wage gap
in South Korea—measured as the difference between median earnings of men and women—is the highest of any OECD country. As of

2013, Korean men had 37 percent higher earnings than women—the highest disparity in all OECD countries—and can be compared with the OECD average of 15.5 percent (OECD 2015). The wage gap is even more pronounced for workers with children. For childless women the wage gap was 13 percent in 2013, but 45 percent between men and women with children. The wage gap also increases with age. For instance, the gender wage gap for women aged 25–29 was 10 percent, but 41.5 percent for women aged 40–44, the highest of any OECD country for that cohort (OECD 2016b). Overall, the wage gap is narrowing slowly: from 40 percent in 2000 to 37 percent in 2013. This can be compared with the OECD average, which fell from 19 percent to 15 percent in this time. The large wage gap discourages Korean women from re-entering the labor force after bearing children. This creates a juxtaposition: nearly two-thirds of women aged 25–34 have a tertiary degree, the second highest of all OECD countries, but the employment rate of Korean women with a tertiary education was the lowest in the OECD in 2014. At the macro level this represents a large economic loss for the country, and for women this results in a loss of lifetime earnings and decreases potential retirement savings through the life course that would eventually feed into a potential second demographic dividend. Keong-Suk Park (2007) found that 20.3 percent of employed women aged 40–55 in 1999 were entitled to receive the National Pension Scheme (NPS) benefits, compared with 79.7 percent of men in the same age cohort. Unfortunately, the twenty-first century has not reversed this trend. As of 2015, 40 percent of female employees were classified as non-regular compared to 26 percent of men. This is critical for women, because less than half (48 percent) of non-regular employees are eligible for the NPS as compared with 98 percent of regular workers (OECD 2016b).

SEX RATIO AT BIRTH

Gender imbalance presents another potential societal cost of South Korea's economic transformation. As has been evident in other Asian countries, most notably China, the sex ratio at birth in South

Korea has been distorted at times. Worldwide the normal sex ratio at birth is 105 boys per 100 girls. As a comparison point for South Korea, the one-child policy in China resulted in sex ratios increasing from 109 boys per 100 girls born in 1982 to a high of 118 in the years 2005 through 2010, although it has declined to 114 in 2016 (Eberstadt 2011; U.S. Census Bureau 2017). Although South Korea does not have a one-child policy, its low fertility rates combined with the cultural importance of having a son and availability of sex-selective technology to terminate unwanted pregnancies—particularly that of female children—resulted in a skewed sex ratio in the 1980s and early 1990s. Den Boer and Hudson (2017) argue that the cultural factor of son preference far outweighs low fertility and sex-selective technology in driving the skewed sex ratio. In other words, low fertility and sex-selective technology in and of themselves are unlikely to result in a skewed sex ratio, particularly in a country that values girls and boys equally.

As seen in Figure 3.5, the Korean sex ratio at birth reached a high of 116.5 boys per 100 girls in 1990 (KOSIS 2014) and has declined since

Figure 3.5.   Sex ratio at birth, South Korea, 1980–2013

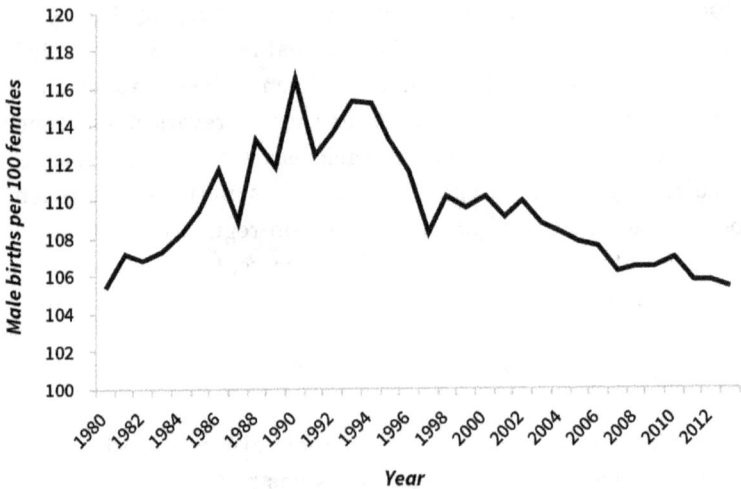

Source: KOSIS (2014).

then, but with a very irregular pattern. The sex ratio at birth in 2014 was 105.3: exactly the same value as that observed in 1980. The overall sex ratio for the country masks variation by birth order; that is, the sex ratio increased with parity as parents utilized sex-selective technology to achieve desired family competition. Den Boer and Hudson (2017) found that between 1981 and 2014 the sex ratio for first births and even second births was nearly at parity, but in the mid-1990s the sex ratios increased to over 200 for women with three children and a sex ratio of 240 was noted for women with four children. The authors also noted higher sex ratios in southeastern Korea where patriarchy and conservative values are strong.

In an attempt to outlaw prenatal sex determination, the Korean government banned prenatal sex identification technologies in 1987 and strengthened policies in 1994. Ultrasound machines to determine the sex of a fetus were banned, and medical personnel could be fined or lose their license for performing such procedures. Concurrently, nongovernmental organizations for women's rights pressured the government to promote the value of daughters as well as sons. Revisions to family law in 1991 reversed some patrilineal practices such as there would no longer be an automatic paternal right to child custody, and daughters/sons would share an inheritance equally (den Boer and Hudson 2017). Even more significant changes were passed in the early 2000s when the traditional hoju system of patrilineal head of family registration was abolished (ibid.).

In a nationally representative survey, Chung and Das Gupta (2007, 16) concluded,

> The decline in the intensity of son preference began amongst the educated professional urban elites, and spread quickly across the rest of the population. This follows the pattern put forward in studies of the collective adoption of new ideas: a slow start, initiated by those with the greater exposure to new information, and then a snowballing of adoption through the population.

The authors argued that normative changes among individuals as a reaction to development brought about the decline in the sex ratios, rather than any policy decisions at the national level. On the other hand, Chung (2013) argued that the International Monetary Fund (IMF) crisis directly disenfranchised workers and the unemployed, which indirectly switched the son preference and patriarchy that had surrounded development and the industrial growth in the country toward daughters. The shift toward balanced sex ratios may be slow as many families still state that they while they expect high educational achievement for sons and daughters, they want their sons to be successful in a profession and daughters to have good spouses (Kong 2013).

The sex ratio imbalance will be felt for years throughout South Korea but particularly as young people start to marry. The middle column of Table 3.1 shows the number of excess males per females in the same age group. Males aged 20–24 in 2014 were born between 1989 and 1994, the apex of the sex ratio curve. The column on the right shows the difference but with females five years younger because men tend to marry women slightly younger than themselves. This heightens the mismatch between males and females because the numbers of children have decreased in each successive cohort because of low fertility. As a result, in 10 years when the current young men aged 20–24 are 30 to 34 years old, or in 15 years when they are 35 to 39 years old, they may face restrictive marriage

Table 3.1.   Difference between the number of males and females by age cohorts, South Korea, 2014

AGE OF MALES IN 2014	EXCESS MALES TO FEMALES SAME AGE GROUP	EXCESS MALES TO FEMALES 5 YEARS YOUNGER
0–4	72,747	-------
5–9	71,816	60,008
10–14	108,971	278,546
15–19	166,258	448,681
20–24	247,979	319,865
25–29	161,680	102,164
30–34	119,068	472,645

Source: KOSIS (2014).

markets. On the other hand, Korean women will be in high demand, or this imbalance may also result in an even greater number of international brides.

THE WORK-FAMILY BALANCE

Many factors have led to sustained low fertility in Korea, as in other Asian countries. The reasons tend to be interlocking, and no one particular factor stands out as a major reason. Strong familism and a patriarchal society have resulted in Korean women having a difficult time reconciling work and parenthood as development and social modernization often clash with traditional roles in the household. In addition to low female labor force participation rates, a gender wage gap, and the higher likelihood for women to participate in nonregular jobs, maternity leave is currently set at 90 days. Women may receive full wages from employers for the first 60 days and then partial or full wages from employment insurance for the remaining 30 days (Chin et al. 2012). Another limiting factor for young mothers is lack of opportunity for part-time work.

Traditionally childcare for children under the age of five in South Korea has been the responsibility of the family. Spending on pre-primary education was 0.2 percent of GDP in 2008, which was the second lowest of the OECD countries (OECD 2012a). Although a new government initiative will enroll all five-year-olds in kindergartens or childcare facilities at no cost to parents, few provisions exist for children under that age. With the shortage of public childcare facilities, the burden for caring for young children generally falls to families, specifically mothers. As the Korean family system has become more nuclear, less of a support network from other relatives exists for childcare. Although the number of childcare facilities is increasing, it is not meeting the demand. Lee (2010) estimates that childcare facilities meet only 30 percent of the need. In 2003, there were 4,405 childcare facilities (public and workplace); by 2007, this had increased to 29,823 (den Boer and Hudson 2017). Even with the rapid increase of facilities, the number of spots available falls far short of demand. As a result, nearly half of all women quit their jobs when they have a child. Mothers supervise all aspects of a child's education: arranging for tutors and for-profit private after school institutions (*hagwons*), meeting with teachers, preparing food and bringing it to their children while they study or in between school and tutoring (Seth 2002).

Even among women who work, house chores and childcare are significant. Working women spend nearly three and a half hours on household chores/childcare on an average working day, which is about seven times as much time as their husbands (Lee 2010). A recent survey showed that although 42.7 percent of Korean men over the age of 13 thought that husbands and wives should share housework evenly, only 16.4 percent reported housework was shared equally (Kim Kyung-rok 2015).

Sorensen (1994, 25) coined the term *corporate families* to describe the Korean family structure with the designated head of the family with specific rights and duties, and then clearly defined roles by all members so there is a succession to the head of the family. This patriarchal system mirrored the capitalist industrial economy of South Korea, and allowed for private families as well as firms to support highly gendered roles and norms (Chang 2013).

In Korean families, children traditionally care for their parents in old age because of filial piety (*hyo*) and the eldest son has the responsibility. This created an intra-household system in which the parents invested heavily in the oldest son, but now parental care has been transferred to the few children in the family. Previously, parents were willing to make economic sacrifices for the son to have every opportunity in the education system so he secured the best possible position. The family system is in a process of change, however, with what Chang (2013) has called the reverse stem family in which the children—even as adults—depend on their middle-aged (or older) parents for housing, prolonged education, and sometimes economic support within the parents' nuclear family.

Tertiary education has become expected of all children; over 80 percent of Korean parents reported in the Programme for International Student Assessment (PISA) survey that they expected their children to obtain at least a tertiary degree (OECD 2013a). Oversight of a child's education traditionally falls to the mother. The Korean mother is highly idealized even in light of the gender differentiation in families; she has a great deal of power within the family, which has been described as skirt wind (*chimabaram*), or a mother with authority (Sorensen 1994, 26). This has also come to refer to a properly educated woman who makes for an ideal daughter-in-law because she not only supervises the child's education but also projects her ambitions onto the children (Seth 2002). This term connotes more than just a support system; these mothers exert true control and have the highest expectations of the children to succeed. A South Korean mother was quoted as saying, "Most Korean mothers want their children to get 100 on all the tests in all the subjects" (Dillon 2008). Mothers wake up early to prepare lunch as well as supper boxes because children may not get home from the hagwons until 10 p.m., depending on the age of the child. Assisting the child in preparation for the college entrance exam is nearly a full-time job for mothers (Harlan 2012). The high costs of childcare and extracurricular education—combined with the change in women's status—have increased the costs to women and families of having a child. However, Korean families remain committed to giving children the highest quality education possible to ensure they are successful in the highly competitive educational system and labor force, which only intensified after the IMF 1997–1998 financial crisis (Eun 2007).

The quest for success has forced some families to dislocate and/or split apart temporarily. Rural mothers and grandmothers have been known to move to an urban area to prepare meals and clean for children/grandchildren who move to the city for perceived superior educational resources. Status for the corporate family system results in a "all for one, and one for all" system where status is conferred to the entire family, not to an individual, thus parents are willing to make extraordinary commitments to the children (Sorensen 1994).

The hyper-competitiveness for educating children is also evident in the Korean phenomenon of goose families (*gireogi gajok*), also sometimes called wild goose fathers or goose mothers. Goose fathers send their wives and children to English-speaking countries, and the fathers visit annually, with the notion that children who are multilingual have a competitive edge (Anderson and Kohler 2012). The number of school-age children living abroad with their mother may be as high as 40,000 (Onishi 2008). Fathers who do not have the resources to visit their children and wives are dubbed penguin fathers. Kim Seong-kon, a professor of English at Seoul National University and president of the American Studies Association of Korea expressed the view that "the unnatural phenomenon of wild geese daddies is a clear sign of something wrong in our society" (Goh-Grapes 2009).

SUMMARY

South Korea's economic success in the second half of the twentieth century and the start of the twenty-first century was aided by a highly educated, urban working-age population, along with an authoritarian developmental governance model that pursued a capital model and was aided by the education dividend. One of the keys for an economy to reap the advantages of the demographic dividend is the investment in human capital to realize economic growth, which is exactly what South Korea did. The economic success, however, was accompanied by seismic cultural shifts often associated with the second demographic transition: a movement away from multigenerational families living together, a retreat from marriage, and low fertility. The Korea case stands out from the European model of the second demographic transition in that nearly all births occur to married couples. Another major, more recent social change in South Korea is that the gendered social structure may be waning, but it is still evident in the M-shaped labor force pattern for women and the work–family imbalance. How South Korea manages social change in tandem with economic change will set the stage for the next period of economic growth and which may usher in a second demographic transition.

4. KOREAN ELDERLY: EMPTY AGING

The demographic dividend, purported to benefit Korea as a whole, has not had positive consequences for most of the current elderly population. At a macro level, the rapid and compressed transformation to a technologically advanced country has been particularly difficult for those aged 65 and above: many of whom lived through the Japanese occupation, some of whom fought in the Korean War, and all of whom experienced the partitioning of their country, rapid urbanization, and industrialization. So, although the elderly population has experienced momentous changes in their lives, nearly half of them now face poverty in the last years and decades of their lives. This compromised economic situation is exacerbated by a low level of social support and overlain by a disintegration of the traditional family structure. The high levels of urban migration of young people have left the South Korean rural elderly with minimal social or government support to combat high levels of poverty. The rapid rise of individualism and the breakdown of the traditional family have accentuated the feeling of loss among many of the elderly. Park (2009) found that the proportion of Korean persons reporting happiness declines steadily with age; two-thirds of those in their 20s and 30s reported being happy, but only one-third of those in their 60s considered themselves happy. For many current elderly Koreans the twilight years are marked by loneliness and isolation rather than by respect and inclusion as an integral part of family and society.

As this chapter describes, the elderly have been affected the most—and the most negatively—by the demographic dividend. The elderly can be defined as those aged 65 or older, which, as of 2017, consists of people born in or before 1952. The older persons in this cohort lived through the Japanese occupation (1910–1945); some were alive in 1937 when the Japanese invasion of Manchuria resulted in a demand for labor, which Korean farmers and laborers first filled voluntarily, but eventually resulted in a forced mobilization of workers. Most of this generation would have been children or young adults in 1944 when 11.6 percent of Koreans lived outside the country, and in 1945 when 2 million Koreans worked in Japan—comprising one-fourth of the industrial labor force at that time (Cumings 2005; Seth 2002). Many of the current elderly were affected by a parent or a family member living outside of the country and the general disruption and destabilization during Japanese colonial rule. In 1947, 1 out of 8 South Koreans returned from working abroad to find their country in economic chaos, but also fueled by optimism and a strong sense of patriotism. Some of the current elderly have also been faced with having family members living in North Korea and are unlikely to have seen them in now over 70 years. Approximately 22,000 people from both Koreas have participated in reunions, with another one planned for 100 people from each side in August 2018. About 71,000 South Koreans, at least half of whom are 80 or older, remain on a waiting list for a chance to meet with relatives in North Korea, but about 3,800 persons on the list die each year without having their wish to see a sibling fulfilled (Choe 2014).

News commentator Tom Brokaw coined the term *the greatest generation* to describe the U.S. generation that grew up during the Great Depression and fought in World War II. Although the timeline shifts forward slightly for the current elderly in South Korea, they, too, could be called the greatest generation, as they suffered tremendously through dislocation and subjugation in their early childhood and/or adulthood, then faced new challenges in adapting to rapid economic and social development in their country. "For instance, young people seem eager to break with the past and aspire to shape a future different from that which their parents and grandparents intended, while their elders seem to be passively disposed to the anomie resulting from the cultural discontinuities and contradictions" (Park and Lester 2008, 22).

Traditionally, care of the elderly has been primarily a family responsibility based on Confucian family values; Palley (1992) argues that South Korea has retained the relational/hierarchical aspects of Confucianism more than any other Asian country. This reliance on family support for care of the elderly has, until recently, led to limited public policy for the Korean elderly. The country's focus on industrial development and economic growth strategies and the belatedness of recent revisions to family law reflect the government's reluctance to involve itself in policy matters related to support of the elderly. Currently, the government provides little to no support to families who care for and share their homes with their elderly parents, other than lower inheritance taxes, but surely this will change as the elderly increase as a percentage of the population.

In addition to declining family support and minimal government transfers, many other circumstances have contributed to the high poverty rates among the current South Korean elderly. For example, low education levels and low migration rates from rural to urban areas limited many elderly persons' participation in the modern industrial era. This has meant fewer elderly were able to accumulate savings through the demographic dividend and participate in pension plans. Figure 4.1 shows how certain circumstances, along with demographic transition forces operated in South Korea, have led to high rates of poverty among the elderly, relative to the remainder of the population. We discuss these circumstances in the following sections.

EDUCATION, URBANIZATION, AND HOUSEHOLD COMPOSITION

Because most of the current Korean elderly were born before 1952, they did not benefit from the phenomenal rise of the Korean educational system. At the end of Japanese occupation in 1945, the illiteracy rate in South Korea was 78 percent (Sorensen 1994). Before liberation, 40 percent of elementary teachers were Japanese, and Korean textbooks were nonexistent (Seth 2002).

Figure 4.1.   Schematic of the first demographic dividend bypassing
the elderly

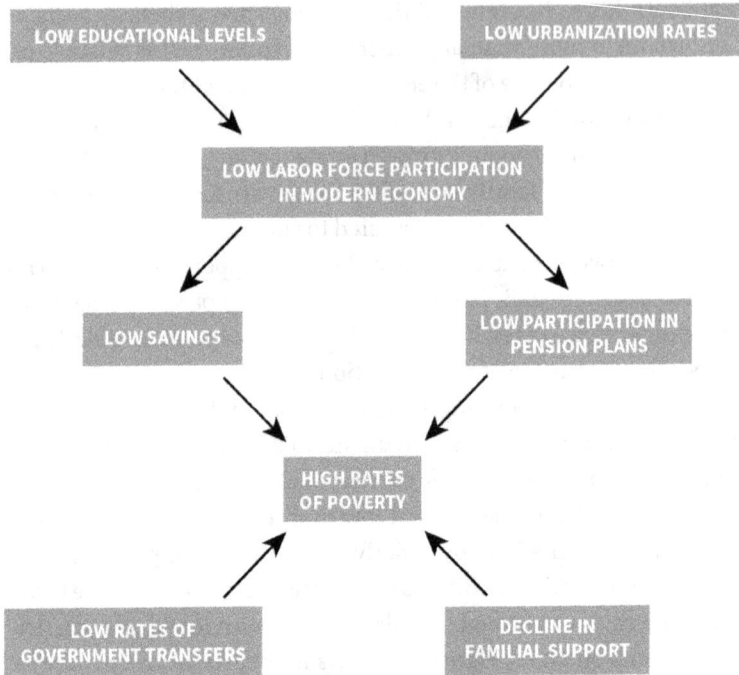

In order to understand the isolation of the rural elderly in South
Korea, it is important to put the entire country into context. In 1960,
just over a quarter (28 percent) of the total Korean population lived
in urban areas, but by 2010 the number increased to 82 percent.
Figure 4.2 shows two trends for the elderly population: (1) the
overall increase in the proportion of the population that is elderly
and (2) the divergence between the rural and urban elderly populations. By 2010, 1 out of 5 rural persons was aged 65 and over, while
only 8 percent of the urban population was elderly. Chang (2013)
refers to this phenomenon as "intergenerationally divided urban
migration."

Until recently, Korean households traditionally included at least
two generations based on the Confucian social contract, which was

Figure 4.2. Percentage of the urban and rural populations aged 65 and over, South Korea, 1960–2010

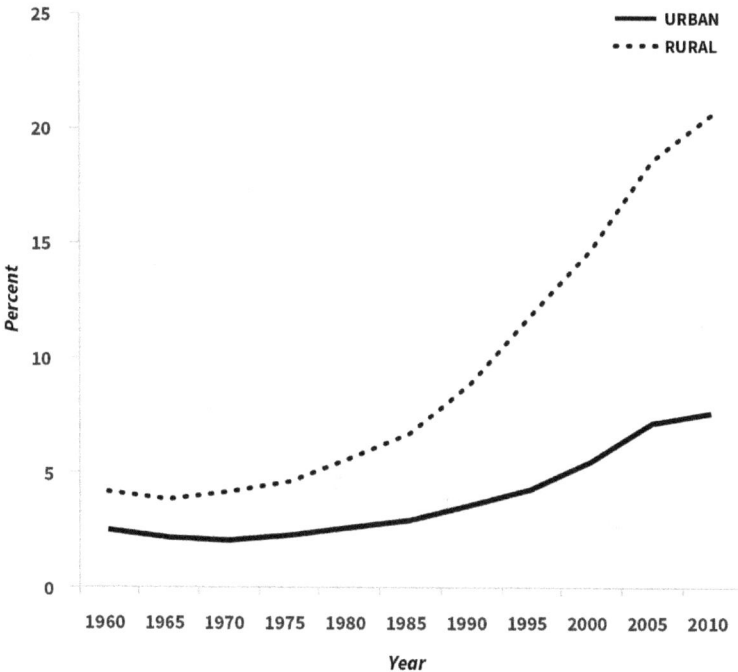

Sources: For 1960–1995: Bell (2004); for 2000–2010: United Nations Databank (2014).

built on the trust that parents would make a large investment in their children's education and, in turn, their children would take care of them in their old age. Figure 4.3 illustrates the changes in South Korean household types over 20 years. One-person households increased from 9 percent of all households in 1990 to 24 percent in 2010, and one-generation households increased from 11 to 17 percent in the same time period. Declines were seen in two-generation households and three-or-more-generation households by 23 and 50 percent, respectively, over this time period.

In addition, as household composition has changed, so has the number of children per household. Families are now smaller so fewer children are available to care for the elderly at home, at a time

Figure 4.3. Percentage distribution of South Korean households by generational composition, 1990–2010

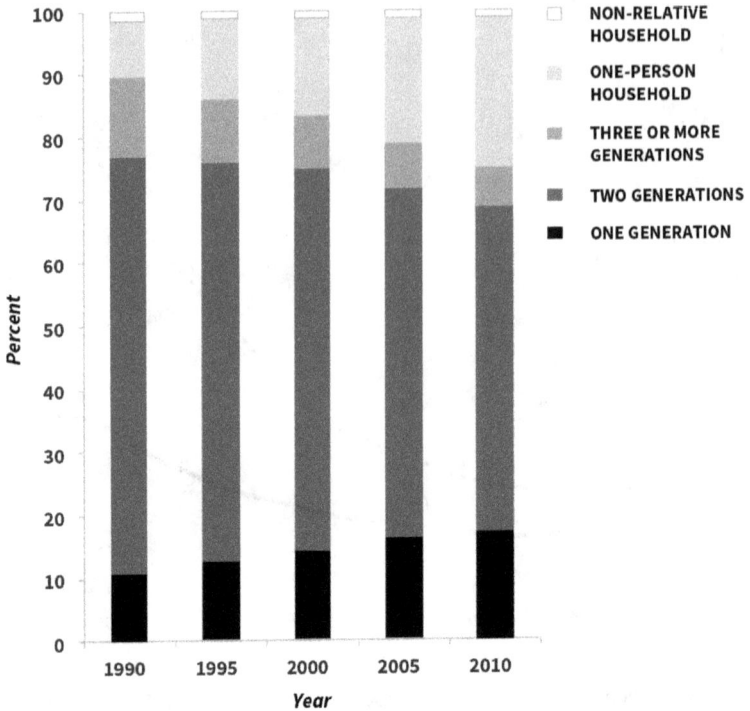

Sources: For 1990–1995: Bell (2004); for 2000–2010: KOSIS (2014).

when the elderly population is growing. Finding elderly care outside of the home in South Korea is rare. As of 1990, only 85 institutional homes provided care to 6,000 elderly persons, and 18 public nursing homes and four privates ones cared for a total of 17,000 persons (Palley 1992). In 2009, approximately 1.1 percent of South Korea's population over age 65 received long-term care in an institution, which is roughly 14 long-term care beds per 1,000 persons over age 65 (OECD 2011a). Although these rates represent a steady increase in institutional care since 2000, in comparison, as of 2008, the United States had 42 long-term care beds per 1,000 persons aged 65 and over, and the OECD average was 44 per 1,000 persons (OECD 2011b).

PENSION PLANS

Virtually no private occupational pension plans exist in South Korea; early pension plans were developed for government employees in 1960, military personnel in 1963, and private school teachers in 1975. A comprehensive public pension plan, the National Pension Scheme (NPS) for private-sector employees was introduced in 1988, but only 10.8 percent of those aged 65 and over currently receive any benefits from the plan, and within that 10.8 percent, many receive only partial payments (OECD 2012b; Shin 2010). In 1988, when the NPS was implemented, it only covered workers in companies with 10 or more employees, which was 26.3 percent of all employed workers. A 1993 revision extended coverage to companies with from five to nine workers, and in 1995 the plan was extended to include rural workers and self-employed workers in urban areas (Keong-Suk Park 2007). Over a third (35.5 percent) of workers were covered by 1995, and when national plans for teachers and government workers are included, 61 percent of the total workforce was covered by 2000.

Currently, the NPS benefits greatly from the demographic dividend of having large cohorts in the working ages, but that advantage will soon shift given the aging population. Pension participants peaked at 18.9 million in 2014, while pension recipients are expected to increase to 11.1 million in 2059, depleting the fund by 2060 (at current contribution and payout rates) (Lee 2010). In part because of the recent introduction of the NPS, public spending on old-age benefits has been quite low: 1.6 percent of gross domestic product (GDP) in 2007, which was only 25 percent of the OECD average (OECD 2012b), but may be as high as 7.3 percent by 2050. When health care and other programs are included, the total cost of benefits to the elderly could exceed 25 percent of GDP by 2050 (Howe, Jackson, and Nakashimi 2007).

To protect against some of these financial concerns, the NPS shifted the entitlement age for benefits to age 61 in 2013 and will phase in an increase to age 65 by 2033 (Klassen and Yang 2010). Also, the current target of paying 60 percent of average career earnings for a worker with 40 years of experience who retires at entitlement age is scheduled to decrease to 40 percent by 2028 (Gordon and Lee 2009; OECD 2012b). Contributions will need to increase even to meet these changes in the plan. South Korea has the highest rates of economically active persons aged 50–64 of any OECD country. This is due in part to the average retirement age of 55 for most employment contracts, which had resulted in a five-year gap for NPS eligibility that, as of 2013, increased to a six-year gap (Phang 2010; Shin 2010).

Given the financial situation, many workers retire from their primary job only to take a second job, which is often self-employment. In 2004, about 60 percent of workers aged 55–64 were self-employed, as were more than three-quarters of workers aged 65 and over (Shin 2010). On average, Koreans work an additional 12 years after they retire from a primary job, owing to the lack of public transfers and declining family support (ibid.). In 2014, Finance Minister Choi Kyung-hwan reported, "About 900,000 retirees flood into the self-employment sector every year, causing cut-throat competition" (Kim 2014). This refers to competition among "mom and pop stores" and small restaurants, which account for nearly two-thirds of start-ups. Many of these small businesses, which were developed by retirees who invested their life savings in the venture, fail within three years. Half of South Korea's self-employed small-business owners are now over the age of 50 (Park 2014). Howe et al. (2007, 14) put it succinctly, "While the demographic transformation has so far been leaning with economic growth, it will begin leaning against it."

Perhaps most troubling is the support ratio—the number of people aged 15–64 per one older person aged 65 or older—which describes the burden placed on the working population by the non-working elderly population. Population growth in South Korea is only expected through 2020 and then will become negative. The workforce itself also is aging; in 2000, about one-quarter of the workforce was aged 50 and over, whereas by 2050 half of the work force will be aged 50 and over (Phang 2005). If labor force participation rates remain at current levels for each age group, the labor force will peak in 2022 with 27.2 million workers, but fall by 21 percent to approximately 21.5 million by 2050 (OECD 2012b). That shift translates to 1.2 persons in the labor force for every elderly person in 2050 as compared with 4.5 in 2010. A challenge for South Korea is finding ways to provide a decent level of support for the elderly without imposing a crushing burden on the working population given the rapidly aging population.

Perhaps it is easiest to envision these demographic dynamics by examining dependency ratios. These can be measured as a youth dependency ratio (population aged 0–14 ÷ population aged 15–64 × 100) and the elderly dependency ratio (population aged 65 and over ÷ population aged 15–64 × 100). The youth and elderly dependency ratios can be added together to get the total dependency ratio. This ratio is an indirect measure of the support structure in a population; it is realized that not everyone aged 15–64 is working, and persons above aged 65 may be working.

As seen in Figure 4.4, the total dependency ratio for South Korea is nearly U-shaped: starting in 1980 at 62, reaching lows in 2000 and 2010 at 39, but then increasing rapidly to 82 by 2050. It would be very deceptive, however, to look at the total dependency ratio without looking at the two components. The youth dependency ratio falls from 55 in 1980 to 19 in 2050, while at the same time the elderly dependency ratio increases from 6 in 1980 to 63 in 2050. The two lines will cross in about 2020; in other words, there will be as many elderly as children in South Korea in about 2020.

This shift in support ratios means that an increasingly larger burden also will be put on the government for old-age benefits. Institutional policy solutions include accelerating the planned increase in the pension eligibility age from the current age of 61 to age 65 by 2033, encouraging workers to stay in their current positions longer before retiring, and increasing the percentage of persons who contribute to the NPS. Although participation is mandatory, 30 percent of the working-age population in 2010 did not contribute to the NPS or any plan (OECD 2012b).

Figure 4.4.   Total, youth, and elderly dependency ratios for
South Korea, 1980–2050

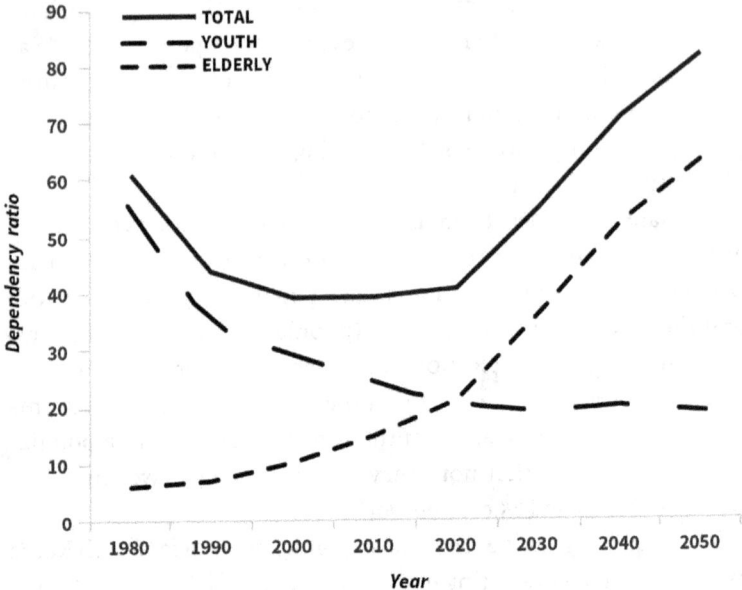

Sources: Phang (2005) and World Bank Database (2015).

Private plans in South Korea include the old mandatory retirement allowance scheme (or severance allowance), introduced in
1953, and new corporate pension plans. The severance allowance is
equal to "one month of wages for every year of service at the rate of
average monthly wage over the last three months prior to depar-
ture" (Klassen and Yang 2010, 7). For companies, this allowance was
beneficial because no other financial provisions were required at
the time of retirement and payment was made from current operating funds. With the increase in the number of elderly persons,
the government is allowing large corporations to augment the NPS
plan with more traditional corporate pension plans, which was a
compromise between business leaders who wanted to abolish the
retirement allowance entirely and labor organizations that sought
to keep it (Klassen and Yang 2010).

POVERTY

Even with these plans in place, the poverty rate of the South Korean elderly is high, particularly for those aged 65 and over who were not able to participate fully in government pension plans and are less likely to co-reside with a child. As of 2016, the relative poverty rate for the Korean elderly was 49.6 percent (OECD 2016b). The OECD defines relative poverty defined as income below 50 percent of the national median household income of the nation after taxes and transfers, adjusted for household size (OECD 2016c). In contrast, as of 2014, only 7 percent of Korean children aged 0–17 lived in poverty. As of 2005, 14 percent of the elderly received government social assistance with monthly benefits averaging less than US$80 per person (Howe et al. 2007).

In addition, because tax rates on labor in South Korea are low based on a policy to boost labor and foreign investment, social spending is also low, particularly for family benefits and measures to reduce poverty. The *Economist* ("What Do You Do" 2011) reports that Korea's tax-benefit system reduces poverty by 18 percent, compared with Sweden's system, which lowers the poverty rate by 80 percent.

Park (2007) argues that labor market segmentation is a major factor in elderly poverty levels. He found those entitled to the NPS are predominantly male, full-time workers, with a high level of education. Net family income for workers entitled to the NPS is about 1.7 times larger than for those workers not entitled to a pension. Furthermore, those entitled to the NPS have financial assets twice that of their peers who will not receive a pension, and their real estate holdings are three times as large. Although access to the NPS greatly improved income for those receiving a benefit, women and irregular/temporary workers were much less likely to receive a pension. Thus, poverty rates mirrored and increased inequities women had already experienced in the labor force. Keong-Suk Park (2007) concluded that elderly poverty is a long-term deprivation resulting from cumulative disadvantages in the labor market and lack of access to pension benefits.

SUICIDE

The rapid integration of South Korea into the global economic structure was accompanied by a shift away from extended family and hometown/local activities to a Western, materialistic, and individualistic approach (Park and Lester 2008). Young people embraced the changes, but the elderly population could not assimilate. One result of this social disarray is the extremely high suicide rates among the elderly.

As recently as 2011, South Korea held the highest suicide rate of any OECD country at 33.3 deaths per 100,000 persons (OECD 2016d). Suicide rates increased by 280.7 percent between 1990 and 2010 in Korea while decreasing in most OECD countries, such as Denmark, Estonia, Hungary, Finland, and Austria experiencing declines of 40 percent or more (OECD 2013b). The only OECD countries with increased suicide rates were Poland, Japan, Russia, Mexico, Chile, and South Korea. Lithuania is the only country with rates near that of South Korea; in 2012 Lithuania's suicide rate (29.5 per 100,000 persons) surpassed that of South Korea (29.1) for the first time.

However, two caveats exist for analyzing a country's mortality rates: (1) differences by age and (2) a need to account for ages in the population structure over time. Because mortality rates vary tremendously by age, a disaggregation of mortality data by broad age groups provide a much clearer picture of mortality patterns in a country. However, comparisons of mortality statistics by age alone can be misleading because changes in the age structure of a population over time are reflected in the rates. For that reason, demographers calculate age-standardized rates so changes in mortality are apparent, as the population age structure is kept constant. As seen in Figure 4.5, age-standardized total mortality declined by 42 percent between 1986 and 2005 for men and 43 percent for women in South Korea (Kwon, Chun, and Cho 2009).

Age-standardized suicide rates, however, rose by 98 percent for males and 124 percent for females, as seen in Figure 4.6, for this same time period (Kwon et al. 2009). When we consider that the overall mortality rate is decreasing in South Korea as was seen in Figure 4.5,

Figure 4.5. Age-standardized mortality rates for South Korean males and females, 1986–2005

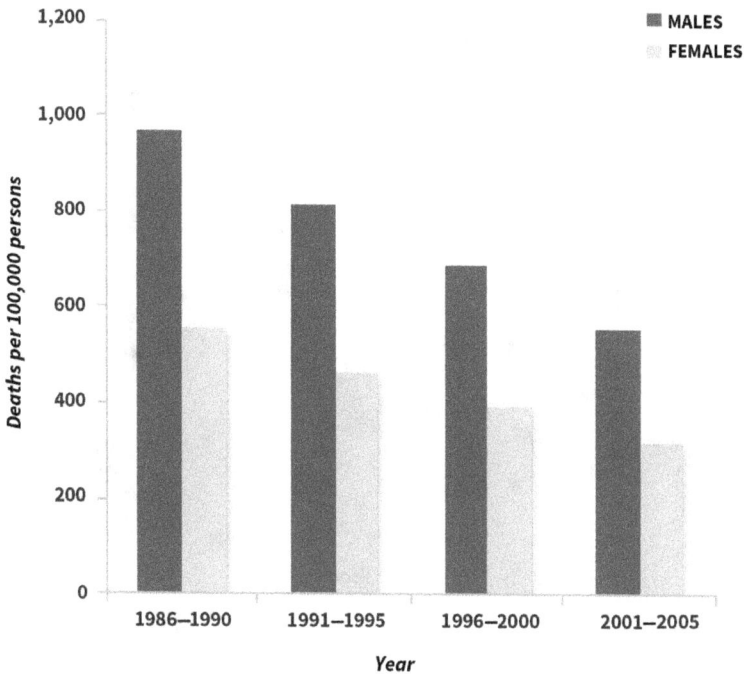

Source: Kwon, Chun, and Cho (2009).

but suicide rates are increasing as seen in Figure 4.6, it is evident that the proportion of deaths as a result of suicide is increasing.

As seen in Figure 4.7, South Korea experienced a spike in suicides following the 1997 IMF economic crisis, when per capita gross national income dropped from US$11,200 in 1997 to $7,400 by 1998 (Kwon et al. 2009). A decline in suicide rates followed the economic recovery, at least for a time, with a decrease from 2000 to 2002. South Korean suicide rates started increasing again, with another dip in 2007 preceding the 2007–2008 global financial downturn, and then increased through 2009. The country's suicide rate bypassed Japan's in 2003, and the gap has increased dramatically with Japan's rates holding fairly steady since 2003. Both Japan and

Figure 4.6.   Age-standardized suicide rates for South Korean males
and females, 1986–2005

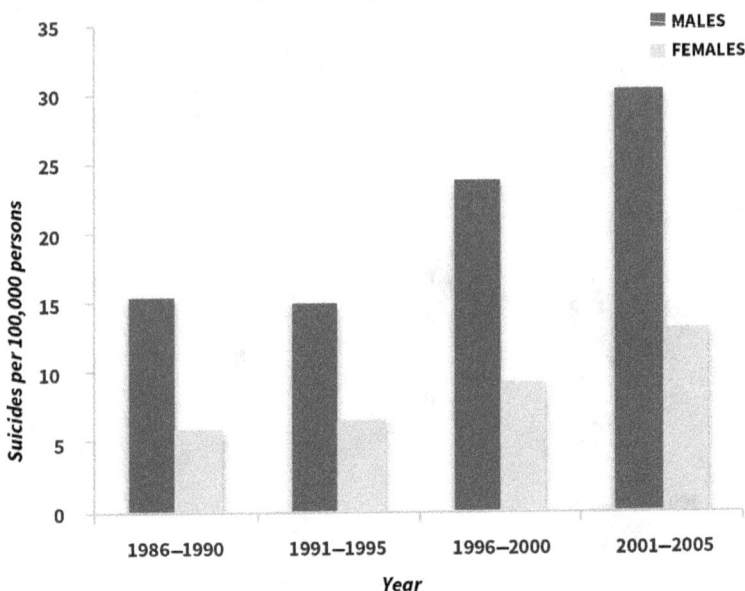

Source: Kwon, Chun, and Cho (2009).

Korea can be contrasted with the OECD average suicide rate, which
started at 17.11 in 1986 but decreased to 13.29 by 2011.

Many articles in the mass media have been written about South
Korea's high suicide rate, but often they focus on youth suicide, or
on unusual events, such as the suicide of a K-pop singer (Stiles 2017)
or a report of Internet-plotted suicides ("Spate of Suicides" 2009). In-
deed, as of 2011, more young Korean people died of suicide than of
any other cause of death. The *Wall Street Journal* reports that a recent
survey conducted by the Korea Health Promotion Foundation found
that, "just over half of South Korean teenagers have suicidal thoughts
this year, while nearly one in three said they had felt very depressed"
(Kang 2014). An OECD (2013b) report noted that treatment for persons with depression and bipolar disease increased by 17 percent
and 29 percent, respectively, between 2006 and 2010, with those
from a lower socioeconomic bracket the most likely to be affected.

Figure 4.7. Suicide rate for South Korea, Japan, and the average for Organization for Economic Cooperation and Development (OECD) countries, 1986–2011

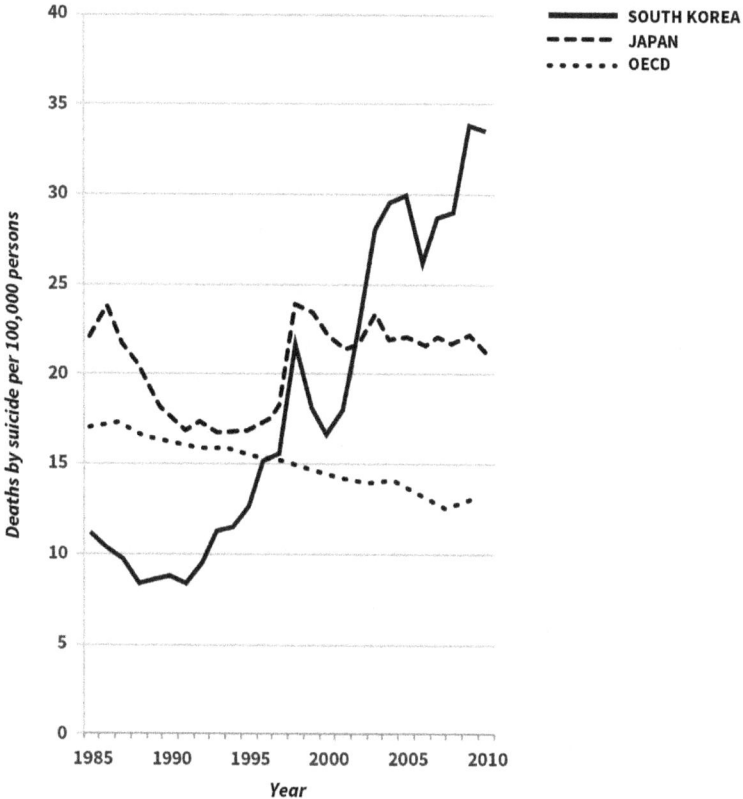

Source: OECD (2013b).

Two unusual aspects about suicide can be seen in South Korea. First is the age pattern. As seen in Figure 4.8, the suicide rate increases exponentially by age—a very different pattern than that of Japan, the United States, or any other OECD country. For example, in 2008, the suicide rate for Koreans aged 75 and older was 160 per 100,000 persons; the OECD average for that age group is 19.3; the country with next highest rate was Hungary at 36.1 (OECD 2009). Second is that suicide rates for Korean women were the highest in

Figure 4.8.   Age-specific suicide rates for South Korea, Japan, and the United States, 2008

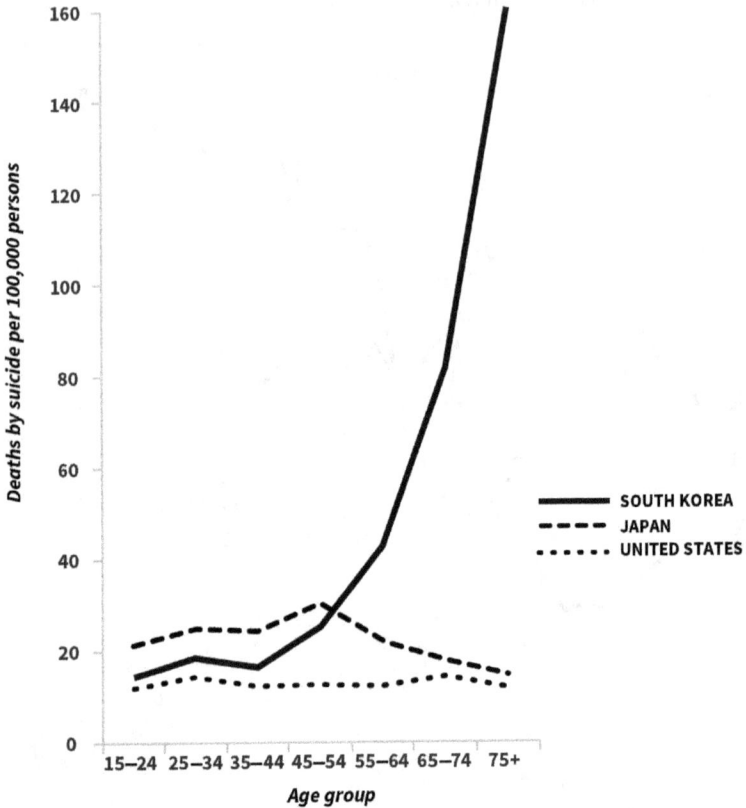

Source: OECD (2009).

the world at 21.4 per 100,000 women (as of 2011), with Japan the next highest at 11.5. The OECD average was 5.92, and the U.S. rate was 4.90 (OECD 2013b).

SHAME AND SELF-RELIANCE

Shame in South Korea reflects not only the shame of a person but also the shame of the family. In a culture that also values self-reliance, mental health problems may be seen as a weakness rather than a disease. On the other hand, suicide may be seen as actually being a self-reliant, altruistic act that lightens the burden one places on others. Park and Lester (2008) note that some elderly people consider suicide an altruistic measure. An elderly person may believe, and state in suicide notes left behind, their suicide would benefit the family by no longer being a financial and emotional drain to the next generation.

The most common methods of suicide for the total Korean population as of 2003 were pesticides/chemicals and hanging/strangulation. These methods alone accounted for nearly three-fourths of Korean suicides (Park and Lester 2008). That pattern is not unusual in countries with low ownership of firearms; Hunt et al. (2010) reported that two-thirds of the suicide deaths in their sample from England and Wales were also caused by hanging or self-poisoning, with poisoning more common among women. The South Korean government recently banned the sale of Gramoxone—one of the most lethal pesticides and easily available in rural areas—with the hope it would halve the suicide rate from pesticides (Normile and Hvistendahl 2012). Korean national death certificates are coded with the cause of death, including intentional death by suicide. Shin et al. (2004) analyzed mortality rates for injuries, including poisoning. Of interest are the age-specific mortality rates for poisoning, which are shown in Figure 4.9. It should be noted that these rates are for all poisoning deaths, not just for suicides.

To determine the age pattern of self-poisoning among pesticide deaths, we can look at data compiled by Lee et al. (2009) for the period 1996–2005 (Figure 4.10). Once again, the increase by age is evident. Kim et al. (2011) were able to interview 388 Koreans who were admitted to an emergency room following self-poisoning. The authors divided respondents into two age groups: elderly (aged 65 and over) and younger (under age 65). Three-quarters of the elderly reported they had a medical illness, and 95 percent were evaluated as depressed. Although 51 percent of the elderly had ingested psychotropic drugs, another 40 percent had ingested pesticides, and 7 percent household products. According to Kim et al. (2011, 983), the most commonly cited reason for the suicide attempt

Figure 4.9.   Mortality rate by poisoning by five-year age groups, South Korea, 2001

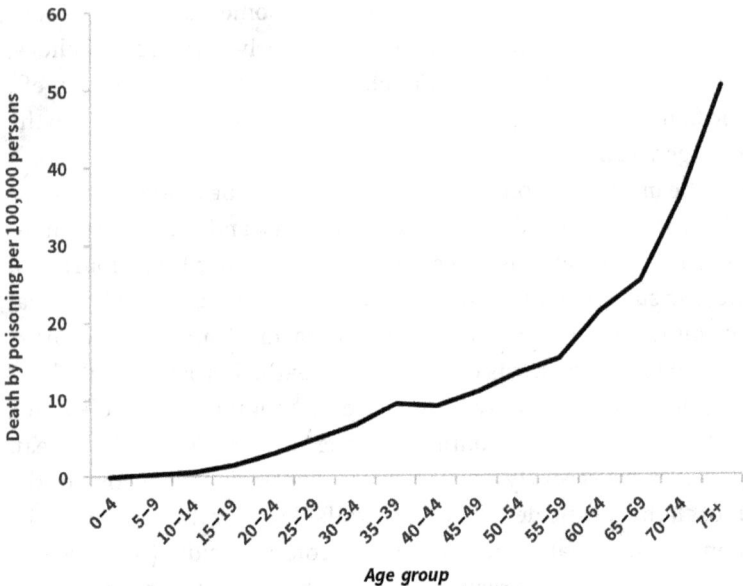

Source: Shin et al. (2004).

was interpersonal problems (40 percent), which the investigators admitted was loosely defined and could include a "breakdown in the social, network, isolation, and loneliness." An additional 26 percent reported that physical illness was the reason for the suicide attempt—a rate nearly five times higher than that of the younger cohort.

Given the link between economic fortunes and suicide rates, it would seem logical that suicide would be most prevalent in cities. However, Lee et al. (2009) estimated that 78.3 percent of self-poisoning deaths from pesticides between 1996 and 2005 occurred in rural areas. This finding is likely related to the relative ease of acquiring pesticides in the provinces where they are available on farms and rarely locked up, and also available for purchase in local stores.

Figure 4.10. Percentage distribution of self-poisoning by pesticide for broad age groups in South Korea, 1996–2005

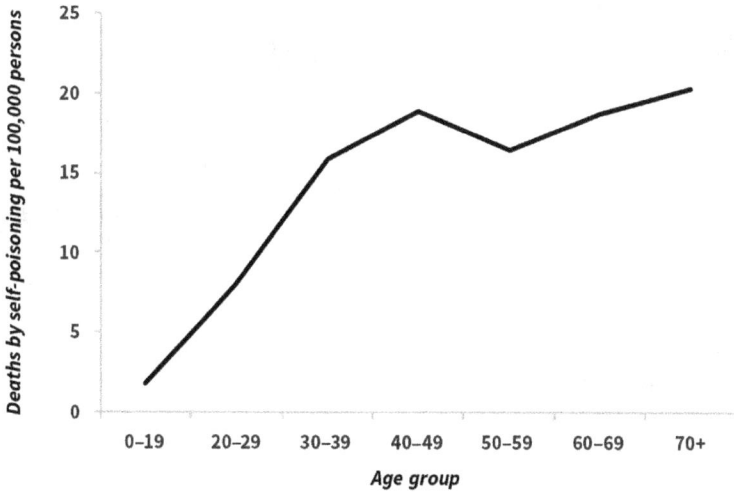

Source: Lee et al. (2009).

As seen in Table 4.1, suicide rates (for the total population and by sex) for Seoul are the lowest in the country, and the metropolitan cities are close to the national average (KOSIS 2013). The provinces, on the other hand, have higher rates than the national averages, with the highest rates in the Gangwon-do with 37.7 suicides per 100,000 persons overall: 52.8 for men and 24.4 for women. A distinguishing feature of Gangwon-do is its low population density (88 persons per square kilometer), the lowest of all Korean provinces. South Korean elderly may be suffering the same fate as Chinese elderly who have been left behind in rural areas and are unable to buy children's respect and support as a result of their diminished role in the family and lack of property (Hvistendahl 2013). Poor health, poverty, and isolation from family members are intertwined, particularly for Korean rural elderly. When we examine population density for administrative units, it is evident that suicide rates are highest in some of the least populated areas such as Gangwon-do.

Table 4.1.   Deaths by intentional self-harm (per 100,000) and
population density (by administrative unit),
South Korea, 2011

DEATHS BY INTENTIONAL SELF HARM PER 100,000			
	TOTAL	MALES	FEMALES	DENSITY (PER SQ. KM)
TOTAL	28.8	41.1	17.9	486
SPECIAL CITIES				
Seoul	24.6	35.5	14.8	16,189
METROPOLITAN CITIES				
Busan	28.6	39.4	19.1	4,452
Daegu	27.5	36.1	20.2	2,767
Incheon	31.2	43.1	20.2	2,588
Gwangju	26.1	36.0	16.9	2,946
Daejeon	29.0	39.7	19.0	2,781
Ulsan	25.5	36.6	16.4	1,022
PROVINCES				
Gyeonggi-do	29.2	41.5	18.4	1,119
Gangwon-do	37.7	52.8	24.4	88
Chungcheongbuk-do	33.6	50.5	18.6	203
Chungcheongnam-do	36.5	52.5	22.0	235
Jeollabuk-do	31.6	49.3	15.4	220
Jeollanam-do	27.8	39.3	16.9	142
Gyeongsangbuk-do	30.0	43.3	17.5	137
Gyeongsangnam-do	29.2	42.5	17.7	300
SPECIAL SELF-GOVERNING PROVINCE				
Jeju-do	28.5	38.1	21.3	288

SQ. KM, square kilometer.
Source: KOSIS (2013).

DEPRESSION AS A RISK FACTOR OF SUICIDE
FOR THE ELDERLY

To determine factors leading to depression in the South Korean elderly I used the 2006 Korean Longitudinal Study of Aging (KLSoA), a

panel study of persons age 45 and older who were residing in households, rather than in a nursing home, hospital, or any such other arrangement. The survey was conducted by the Korean Labor Institute (2007). Respondents were also given a medical examination; those data are available in the 2006 wave. The Employment Insurance Fund provided funding for the survey, which was conducted by the Korea Labor Institute. Interviews were conducted using Computer Assisted Personal Interviewing (CAPI).

Of the 7,574 households selected in the 2006 KLSoA study with an eligible respondent (aged 45 and over), 6,171 interviews were completed for a response rate of 81 percent. The 1,403 non-interviews were refusals. For the purpose of this analysis, the sample was limited to all persons aged 65 and over, for an N of 3,518.

Two dependent variables were used for two separate logistic analyses: (1) a self-report of depression (Have you ever had feelings of being sad, blue, or depressed for two weeks or more during the past year?); and (2) a medical doctor's assessment of depression using the Center for Epidemiologic Studies Short Depression Scale (CES-D10: Standard Depression Status). Because fewer respondents received the medical doctor's assessment, the N for that portion of the analysis dropped to 3,488.

Two sets of models were run. Variables used in the first set were age, sex, urban status, marital status, education, have a child, receive aid from a child, co-reside with a child, currently working, and health status. All independent variables were dichotomies; for instance, age is a dummy variable coded as 1 for ages 65–74 and 0 for ages 75 and over.

In the second set of models, two economic variables were added: (1) assets, which is a dichotomous measure of whether the respondent had assets above or below the mean of 11,709,000 won, and (2) income, measured as whether the respondent had an income above or below the mean of 769,000 won. The variables relating to children (if they had any, if they received any aid from any child, and whether they co-resided with any child) were deleted, and in their place two social isolation indices were created. The first isolation index measured whether the respondent had any friends or family they saw

Table 4.2.   Sample characteristics of the Korean Longitudinal Sample of Aging used in this analysis, 2006

VARIABLE	PERCENTAGE
Aged 65–74	64.9
Female	57.7
Live in a city	51.4
Currently married	63.2
High school or more	19.7
Have at least one child	97.5
Do not receive aid from any child	25.0
Co-reside with a child	8.4
Currently work	15.0
Fair or poor general health	70.3
Assets (below mean of 11,709,000 won)	48.0
Income (below mean of 769,000 won)	63.2
Friends or family not seen regularly	14.2
Limited frequent social group participation	39.2
Self-report of depression	15.7
Medical report of depression	44.4
N	3,518

Author's analysis of data from the 2006 Korean Longitudinal Sample of Aging (Korean Labor Institute 2007) for aged 65 and over cohort.

regularly; the second variable measured whether the respondent was a part of any social group that met frequently.

The percentage of respondents reporting each characteristic is shown in Table 4.2. Compared to the overall Korean population a much smaller percentage of the studied population lives in cities: the sample is 51.4 percent urban versus 81.5 percent of the total population in 2006 (World Bank 2017). Another variable in which the sample differs from the Korean population as a whole is education. Just under 20 percent (19.7 percent) of the sample has a high school degree or more. As of the year 2000, 42 percent of Koreans aged

25–64 had attained a tertiary education. Among Koreans aged 25–34 years old, two-thirds (66 percent) had completed tertiary education, the highest share among OECD countries, compared with an average of 39 percent (OECD 2014). As expected in a survey of the elderly, the sample included more women than men and showed a low percentage of working respondents. Virtually everyone in the sample (97.5 percent) had at least one child. Nearly two-thirds (63 percent) of the sample had an income below the mean income level, and 48 percent had assets below the mean for assets. Most people (86 percent) saw friends and/or family on a regular basis, but 39 percent said they did not participate frequently in any group activities. Doctors coded nearly three times as many people as being depressed (44.4 percent) as those who self-reported depression (15.7 percent). This disparity is not surprising given the stigma surrounding mental health in South Korea.

Results from the logistic regressions are shown in Table 4.3. For values less than one, this means that persons in that category are less likely to have depression. So, for instance in model 1, currently married people are 44 percent (1.00 – 0.56) less likely to self-report depression than non-married respondents. For values over one, persons in that category are more likely to report depression than the comparison category. For instance, persons in fair or poor health are 3.43 times more likely to self-report depression than others in good or excellent health. Looking first at models 1 and 2 in which the dependent variables are self-report of depression and medical report of depression, respectively, there are three significant variables across both models: marital status, education, and health. In addition, city was also significant in model 2, or in other words, urban residents are 20 percent (1.00 – 0.80) less likely to have a medical report of depression than rural residents. Currently married respondents were about half as likely to be depressed as those not currently married: 44 percent (1.00 – 0.56) less likely for self-reported depression and 43 percent (1.00 – 0.57) less likely for doctor's report of depression. Persons with at least a high school education were 15 percent (1.00 – 0.85) less likely to report being depressed than people with less than a high school education, and half as likely to be coded as

Table 4.3.   Adjusted odds ratio and confidence intervals
for depression among South Korean elderly aged 65
and over, 2006

CHARACTERISTIC	SELF-REPORT OF DEPRESSION, MODEL 1	MEDICAL REPORT OF DEPRESSION, MODEL 2	SELF-REPORT OF DEPRESSION, MODEL 3	MEDICAL REPORT OF DEPRESSION, MODEL 4
Aged 65–74	1.14 (0.93–1.41)	0.99 (0.84–1.16)	1.15 (0.93–1.41)	0.99 (0.84–1.16)
Female	1.19 (0.93–1.51)	1.04 (0.87–1.24)	1.19 (0.93–1.51)	1.04 (0.87–1.24)
Live in a city	0.90 (0.74–1.09)	0.80 (0.69–0.92)**	0.90 (0.74–1.09)	0.80 (0.69–0.93)*
Currently married	0.56 (0.45–0.69)**	0.57 (0.48–0.68)**	0.56 (0.45–0.69)**	0.57 (0.48–0.67)**
High school or more	0.85 (0.63–1.16)*	0.54 (0.43–0.67)**	0.85 (0.63–1.16)	0.54 (0.44–0.67)**
Have at least one child	1.07 (0.61–1.86)	0.75 (0.43–1.29)	----	----
Receive aid from at least one child	1.33 (1.05–1.67)	1.13 (0.94–1.36)	----	----
Co-reside with a child	0.70 (0.46–1.08)	0.99 (0.72–1.37)	----	----
Currently work	0.81 (0.59–1.11)	0.84 (0.67–1.04)	0.89 (0.64–1.22)	0.92 (0.74–1.16)
Fair or poor health	3.43 (2.59–4.54)**	3.28 (2.76–3.89)**	3.23 (2.44–4.28)**	3.15 (2.65–3.75)**
Assets	----	----	1.04 (0.86–1.26)	1.01 (0.87–1.17)
Poverty	----	----	1.23 (1.00–1.53)	1.28 (1.10–1.50)*
Limited friends/family	----	----	1.35 (1.04–1.75)*	1.29 (1.04–1.61)*
Limited group interaction	----	----	1.41 (1.15–1.73)**	1.49 (1.28–1.75)**
N	3,516	3,488	3,516	3,488
Log-likelihood	–1,431.37**	–2,171.99**	–1,420.84**	–2,147.71**

*$p < .05$
**$p < .001$
Author's analysis of data from the 2006 Korean Longitudinal Sample of Aging
(Korean Labor Institute 2007) for aged 65 and over cohort.

depressed by a doctor. Those in fair or poor health were more than
three times as likely to be depressed than those in good health
(models 1 and 2).

The deletion of the child-related variables in models 3 and 4 (see
Table 4.3) resulted in fairly consistent odds ratios for the variables

in both models. For instance, people with at least a high school education were 46 percent (1.00 – 0.54) less likely to have a doctor's diagnosis of depression in models 2 and 4. Marriage and health remained the key variables; the only income/asset variable to reach significance was the low-income variable in model 4, where those with income below the mean were 28 percent more likely than respondents with income above the mean to have a medical report of depression. The two social isolation variables were significant in both models 3 and 4. Respondents who have limited interaction with a social group were 41 percent and 49 percent more likely to be depressed (respectively for models 3 and 4) than those who have more frequent social group contact; the importance of the friend or family variable was less significant, but persons with limited contact with close friends or family were roughly 30 percent more likely to be depressed than those with more frequent contact.

These results were expected, but it was surprising that no effect was found for having a child, receiving aid from a child, or co-residing with a child in the first set of models. The effects of income and assets were minimal in the second set. Married respondents who were in good health, saw friends or family frequently, or belonged to social groups were less likely to be depressed, and being in a city decreased the odds of depression, as diagnosed by a doctor.

These results indicate the complexity of trying to understand the high suicide rates among Korean elderly by using depression as a proxy and a set of variables that model their interactions with family, friends, and the greater society. The elderly included in the 2006 KLSoA study (Korean Labor Institute 2007) were not the beneficiaries of the incredible education fever discussed in Chapter 2, and as of 2005, more than two-thirds of the elderly population (71.4 percent) had an elementary school education or less (Kim et al. 2010). The economic and development changes in South Korea were accompanied by the rapid transformation of families: the nuclear family becoming the norm, with most families having one or two children. Although it is not surprising that the elderly who feel left behind—either living in rural areas and/or having little interaction with their children and grandchildren—are depressed, the high elderly suicide rates are a poignant reminder of the failure of the demographic dividend to benefit South Korea's elderly population.

SUMMARY

The Korean elderly who are unable to participate in the mainstream economy for whatever reason and lack regular income, including transfers from family or government, may experience what is termed *empty aging* (Chang 2013). Although some elderly who live alone may receive financial and/or emotional support from their families, many are in poor health, live in poverty, and may not be eligible for government subsidies.

One of the challenges facing South Korea is how to sustain economic growth in the future while at the same time providing more assistance to the elderly. It is a Herculean task to continue economic growth and at the same time to provide for the elderly, particularly during a period of time with a shrinking workforce population. South Korea must address these issues head-on, now, while there are solutions available. While there are geopolitical and economic policies that can be and should be put into place, in the following chapter I focus on the demographic solutions that should be considered in the constellation of options.

5. POLICY OPTIONS

This chapter assesses whether and how future demographic and social policies in South Korea might be able to help the nation cope with looming slowdowns in economic growth. Assessments delve into the demographic and socioeconomic drivers and consequences of economic growth and their differential distributional consequences, including first and second demographic transitions and their consequences.

Although the optimistic scenario of a second demographic dividend has not yet actually occurred, one cannot dismiss the hypothesis that lowered child dependency and increased life cycle savings could be factors in producing a second demographic dividend. The education dividend, which was so important for South Korea's first demographic dividend, has perhaps reached a saturation point. With such high rates of tertiary education in the country, it is hard to imagine education will impact productivity, health, and general well-being as strongly as it did during the first demographic dividend. Thus, other demographic changes may play an increasingly important role in tandem with economic and social policies to maintain the levels of economic growth already achieved in South Korea. For this to happen, the South Korean government must institute policies sooner rather than later.

To foster a second demographic dividend (as defined earlier in terms of a country being able to maintain previously achieved levels of economic growth), decreases in the size of the Korean labor force must be forestalled. We have seen throughout the book how sustained low fertility in South Korea over the last 30-plus years has resulted in smaller cohorts of children and will soon also create

Table 5.1. Summary of policy recommendations for South Korea to achieve the second demographic dividend to benefit the elderly

MAIN FINDING	KEY RECOMMENDATIONS
INCREASE FERTILITY RATES	
Between 1995 and 2002 fertility declined from 1.65 children per woman to 1.17, from which point the TFR has hit a plateau with minor variations from year to year.	1. Increase parental leave (maternal and paternal) by enforcing compliance and raising the benefit level/length of time; government should pay 100% pay for father for the first month. Government should continue/increase subsidization of SMEs for hiring temporary workers. 2. Enhance childcare quality and provide more childcare centers. Require accreditation of childcare centers. 3. Provide housing subsidies for young families, with a sliding scale for the number of children in the family. 4. Promote gender equality and a balance of family-work life through flexible hours and/or telecommuting where possible.
INCREASE FEMALE LABOR FORCE PARTICIPATION RATES	
Female labor force attachment is very low in South Korea. • Women retreat from the labor force during their 30s to have their families, begin to rejoin the labor force in their 40s, and end their labor force participation in their 50s, which accelerates in their 60s. • As of 2013, Korean men had 36.6 percent higher earnings than women.	1. Continue the Best Family Friendly Management certifications, which provide various incentives and government certifications for companies that have family-friendly policies for both men and women. 2. Promote gender equality in all aspects of family life, including the number of hours men spend on housework and childcare. 3. Expand the Women's Resource Academy to encourage and train more women to be effective managers. 4. Expand the Women's Resources Database to fill more entry-level (and return) positions. 5. Maintain a government task force on family and gender equality; work to implement the task force findings.
INCREASE RATES OF IMMIGRATION	
There are an estimated 500,000 legal immigrants working in South Korea, and perhaps as many as 300,000 undocumented workers. Most immigrants enter Korea either as quasi-guest workers or for international marriages.	1. Develop a labor-based immigration system for permanent migration that also allows families to migrate. 2. Increase the number of multicultural centers for families. 3. Continue and increase social cohesion policies for acceptance of immigrants and multicultural families.
INCREASE PRODUCTIVITY AND LENGTHEN WORK LIVES	
South Korea's labor productivity level was 1% in the 2011-2015 period, with annual productivity growth in the service sector only 2% from 1980 to 2010; the service sector's productivity was less than half (45%) that of the manufacturing sector in 2014.	1. Reduce family debt. 2. Increase innovation in the service sector. 3. Increase productivity in SMEs. 4. Expand education/training opportunities for older workers.
RAISE POPULATION GROWTH THROUGH REUNIFICATION WITH NORTH KOREA	
14% of North Korean men and 8% of females (aged 15+) have a tertiary education; 43% of South Korean men and 36% of women aged 25-64 have a tertiary education.	Plan for the education and training of North Koreans; the workforce will be helpful in raw numbers but will need extensive training.

SME, small and medium enterprise; TFR, total fertility rate.

smaller cohorts of people in the working ages. Thus, for any hope of a second demographic dividend, South Korea must maintain the size of its working-age population. Table 5.1 summarizes five ways in which policy changes now could help address the supply of workers in the near and distant future: (1) increase fertility rates; (2) increase female labor force participation rates; (3) increase immigration; (4) increase productivity and lengthen work lives; and (5) raise population growth through reunification with North Korea. For each aspirational goal, the current status of each is shown on the left column of the table and potential policy options that might optimize social and demographic factors that would help generate a second demographic dividend and maintain growth are listed on the right. Several of the policy options can impinge on more than one category, and so the most efficacious approach is likely to be multifaceted in nature. In the following sections, each major policy option is discussed.

INCREASE FERTILITY RATES

South Korea reached below-replacement fertility in 1983, thus instigating concerns about the implications of low fertility for the country's continued economic dynamism. The decline in the total fertility rate (TFR) in South Korea was pronounced between 1980 and 1984 when it dropped from 2.83 children per woman to 1.76. Fertility further declined from 1.65 children per woman to 1.17 between 1995 and 2002, after which point only minor variations have occurred from year to year. The TFR nadir was reached in 2005 at 1.08, but it rebounded to 1.3 in 2012 (KOSIS 2015) and declined again to 1.2 in 2013 and 2014, and in 2015 and 2016 it was estimated to be 1.3 (U.S. Census Bureau 2016).

Pronatalist policies such as the Saeromaji plan introduced in 2006 have had virtually no effect on South Korea's TFR, making it evident that no simple solution exists for increasing fertility in South Korea; a multifaceted approach that addresses a range of economic and social factors will be needed to stave off worries about the consequences of very low rates of childbearing. One principal concern involves the perception that the country must do everything it can to prevent the economy from shrinking. That is, policymakers must not only try to avoid recessions, but also guard against long-term shrinkage in the economy from population decline.

The very low fertility rate in South Korea is thus viewed as a great concern for the economic and demographic health of the country. Raising fertility, of course, would provide no guarantee of sufficient economic growth. Choe and Cho (2008) have been optimistic that there is a high likelihood of success in enhancing fertility levels given that some causes of the lowest low levels have been rapid and recent, and given that South Korea has been successful in dealing with population issues in the past, such as achieving a rapid decline from high to below replacement fertility and success in reversing an imbalanced sex ratio. Nine years after the publication of their paper there is less hope for optimism as evidenced by the lack of a fertility turnaround to date, but South Korea has shown itself time and time again to be a resilient country.

Increasing fertility levels will require long-term planning and will not be easy to accomplish. Job tenure is highly sought by well-educated Koreans and may be a requirement in the minds of many young people to establish households, marry, and have children. Elimination of barriers to a first-career position is a critical step in increasing marriage rates and maintaining or lowering the mean ages of marriage and childbearing. Given the high levels of college graduation in South Korea and that nearly all childbearing takes place within marriage, decreasing entry-level labor market insecurity must be a high priority. Otherwise a restructuring of the economy—rather than a cyclical phenomenon—may have a negative effect on childbearing and marriage.

Parental leave is underutilized in South Korea for both mothers and fathers. Although women's jobs are protected by law while they take maternal leave, nearly 4,000 female workers were terminated during family leave between 2010 and 2012. An even greater concern, though, is the small percentage of women who use maternity leave. In 2012, only 19.3 percent of South Korean mothers used maternity leave, as compared with France where 97 percent of eligible mothers took advantage of maternity leave in 2007, and Germany where 73 percent of eligible women used maternity leave in 2001 (Myunghwa Lee 2015).

As of October 2014, parental leave in South Korea for each parent is 40 percent of his/her full-time income or 60 percent if the parent chooses to work part-time, and 100 percent for the first month of the second parent's use with a ceiling of approximately US$1,400 (Lee and Myunghwa 2015). Even though mothers and fathers are entitled to equal amounts of childcare leave, just 3,421 men took advantage of the right in 2014, although that was nearly double the 1,790 men who took the benefit in 2012 (Park 2015).

In addition to parental leave, other pronatalist policies involve increasing housing subsidies for larger families and improving childcare options. The Korean government has addressed housing in a variety of ways. For example, housing benefits implemented in July 2015 were designed to ensure every person is able to meet minimum living costs. "Housing finance programs through the National Housing Fund offer affordable mortgages to assist home purchases by moderate- to middle-income households" (Kim and Park 2016, 17). The existing programs would be even more effective if housing assistance increased with the number of children in a family. Not only are the numbers of available childcare centers low, the quality is of great concern to parents. "Waiting lists of more than a year plague state-run centers that are cheaper and better maintained than private ones, with official data in September showing as many as 98,000 children were in line for a place in government centers that account for 5 percent of the country's daycare facilities" (Christine Kim 2015). The government must address the questions and answers (Q&A) of childcare: quality and availability. Currently, the government is failing on both counts.

INCREASE FEMALE LABOR FORCE PARTICIPATION RATES

Labor force participation for Korean women remains very low compared to women in other Asian and developed countries, but the reversal of long-standing labor practices would positively impact addressing the potential benefits of the second demographic dividend. As seen in Chapter 3, the weak attachment of Korean women to the labor force starts a vicious cycle in which women find it difficult to build stable careers, which limits later employability and perpetuates stereotypes of women as inferior labor (Keong-Suk Park 2007). Adding more women to the labor force would have a triple benefit of: (1) increasing the number of workers paying into the current NPS system, (2) raising the likelihood of households' amassing savings during the working years, and (3) increasing the number of women qualifying for benefits by retirement age. As might be expected, policies for increasing female labor force participation are interrelated with policies that need to be in place to increase fertility; otherwise female labor force participation could result in a decline in fertility.

Increasing women's workforce participation also depends on increasing gender equality, which may be the most difficult aspect of Korean culture to change. Gender stratification is institutionalized throughout the Korean family and society, and is reinforced by Confucian traditions resistant to change. Gender equality issues affect fertility rates as well as female labor force participation rates. The Korean Ministry of Gender Equality and Family (MoGEF) is focusing on ways of achieving work–family life balance for women and men. One program is called the Best Family Friendly Management certification program, which offers incentives and government certificates to companies that offer family-friendly policies for both men and women. As of December 2015, 1,363 corporations and organizations acquired the certification based on policies for parental leave, childcare, and/or flextime. In addition, workers are encouraged to depart their workplace on time every Wednesday to spend time with their families. The government campaign is a small step to encourage workers to spend time with family in spite of a busy work life.

The MoGEF states on its web page that it has established a five-year plan to address gender equality policies. Seven main projects are: (1) promotion of a culture of gender equality, (2) promotion of work–family life balance, (3) addressing the gender gap in employment, (4) greater representation of women in public fields, (5) eradication of violence and protection of human rights, (6) improvement of health and welfare, and (7) promotion of a stronger policy platform to pursue gender equality. This is an ambitious agenda and one that requires movement on all policies at once to effect change, but it is evident the government is concerned about the negative consequences of gender inequality at both the micro and macro levels.

INCREASE IMMIGRATION

Immigration to South Korea has been minimal in recent decades but could become a positive factor in increasing the size of the workforce population. There are an estimated 500,000 legal immigrants working in South Korea, and perhaps as many as 300,000 undocumented workers. South Korea is known for having a homogenous population, and it has not been known as a receiving country for migrants. Starting in the 1980s labor shortages appeared in certain sectors of the economy: the 3D jobs of dangerous, dirty, and demeaning. Immigration policy at the time was restricted to employment of foreign nationals in professional or entertainment occupations, but very little enforcement existed to prevent immigrants from working in other sectors of the economy. Chinese people of Korean descent (Joseonjok) were ideal migrants in the late 1980s because their ethnicity was more or less similar to the native-born Korean population. Because they came from impoverished regions such as the Yanbian Autonomous Prefecture in China, they were willing to accept the 3D jobs (Lim 2008), particularly in the manufacturing and construction industries. In 2007, the Ministry of Justice introduced the Work Visit (H-2) visa, which granted multiple entries and work permits for ethnic Koreans with foreign citizenship for employment only in industrial fields such as agriculture, small- and medium-sized manufacturing, construction, or the service industry (Library of Congress 2013).

A next step in Korean immigration law was the Industrial Training System, started in the 1990s, in which temporary foreign workers were treated as trainees rather than as legal laborers. Undocumented workers increased under this system, and up to 70 percent of trainees left their training positions to be employed in more lucrative positions elsewhere in South Korea (Lim 2008). The Employment Permit System replaced the Industrial Training System in 2004, with the development of an E-9 visa for employment of nonprofessional foreign workers (Library of Congress 2013). This system allowed employers to hire foreign workers in industries with labor shortages, such as agriculture and stockbreeding, fisheries, construction, and manufacturing. But because the "workers" were trainees, they were denied basic labor rights of unionization and were given low wages. Trainees also had time limits on their visas: for one year at the start of the program, and eventually three years. One extension for up two years is now possible, but permanent residency is not allowed for E-9 visa holders.

During the financial crisis in the 1990s the number of unemployed Koreans increased from approximately 660,000 in 1997 to 1.8 million in February 1999 (Lim 2008), which prompted some politicians to call for an end to immigration so that Koreans could fill those jobs. Many Koreans, however, preferred to remain unemployed rather than taking a 3D job.

Because fertility is likely to remain low in South Korea, immigration is critical for growth in the labor force and needs to be addressed in both policy and in the narrative of the country. South Korea will need to move past a guest-worker migration system to allow immigrants to stay permanently and become incorporated into the country. Also, greater attention will need to be paid to integration of families created through international marriages, and, in particular, to the acceptance and integration of children from international marriages. The MoGEF has disclosed plans to aid multicultural families including hiring of 1,400 people to assist multicultural elementary students with Korean language services. In addition, the monitoring of marriage brokers will be tightened to identify fraud. A third area of focus on international marriages is monitoring domestic violence, which often results from a lack of knowledge of each other's culture and language. An additional 12 multicultural centers are planned to be set up to provide better support for international brides as the numbers have grown from 170,000 brides in 2009 to 220,000 in 2012 (Ministry of Gender Equality and Family 2016).

INCREASE PRODUCTIVITY AND LENGTHEN WORK LIVES

Productivity in its most simple terms is units of output per unit of input. Productivity measurement focuses on how to get more units of output (goods produced or services rendered) for each unit of input (materials, labor hours, machine time) than competitors are able to deliver (Chew 1988). Although South Korea historically has had a high labor productivity level, it slowed to 1 percent in the 2011–2015 period. Productivity also is uneven among sectors, with annual productivity growth in the service sector being only 2 percent from 1980 to 2010, a much lower level than the manufacturing sector's rate of 8 percent (Jong-Wha Lee 2015). And in 2014, the service sector's productivity was still less than half (45 percent) that of the manufacturing sector (OECD 2016b). In comparison, the Organization for Economic Cooperation and Development (OECD) average of service sector to manufacturing productivity was 90 percent in 2014. This gap is critical in South Korea because 70 percent of the labor force works in the service sector. Several factors contribute to the gap between the two sectors. First, South Korea relies on exports, which have expanded from 15 percent of the gross national income in 1970 to 56 percent in 2013. This reliance on exports has made South Korea's economy more vulnerable to changes in external demands (Jong-Wha Lee 2015). Second, the export-based economy has drawn innovation and resources from the service sector to the manufacturing sector. Third, the service sector in South Korea is dominated by small and medium enterprises (SMEs), with governmental policies that have tended to ensure the survival of small firms rather than increase overall productivity.

Even with higher levels of immigration, increasing productivity will be key for economic growth; to do this South Korea must address both demand-side and supply-side issues. On the demand side, South Korea must address its increasing level of household debt, which currently stands at more than 160 percent of household income (Mundy 2016). Household debt in South Korea has risen steadily for more than three decades and is seen as one of the economy's weakest points. On the supply side, South Korea must implement structural reforms to stimulate productivity growth, which should

> emphasize the development of modern services industries, including health care, education, telecommunications, business processing, and legal and financial services. Efforts to ease product regulations and lower barriers to foreign investment would promote competition and technological innovation. South Korea must also dismantle the obstacles that start-up businesses face. To this end, the government must redress shortcomings in the venture-capital market, nurture the labor force's skills, and encourage entrepreneurship. It must also confront the huge, family-controlled chaebols—such as Hyundai, LG, and Samsung—that contributed significantly to rapid industrialization and technological advancement but also block competition from start-ups and SMEs, stifling dynamism and innovation. (Jong-Wha Lee 2015)

Park and Shin (2012, 27) argue that "the [service] sector has been acting as an absorber of surplus workers who are unable to find productive employment in the face of the structural transformation. Since many of those workers end up in marginal, low-productivity, low-wage service jobs, this brings down the productivity of the service sector." Noland (2011) echoes this concern that the government has set up entry barriers for both new domestic and international competitors, which is exacerbated by government subsidization of existing SMEs that dominate the service sector. The appropriate policy should not slow down the manufacturing sector, but rather assist in the structural shift from manufacturing to services. Other options include government subsidization of training programs for dislocated workers from the manufacturing sector or older workers who want to extend their work career. Traditionally, government policy has served to protect SMEs and SME jobs, which has worked to stifle innovation and reduce competition. It will be difficult to turn around these policies to foster innovation, but it will be incumbent on the South Korean government to do so if it wants to bring the service sector into parity with the manufacturing sector by upgrading the service sector and fostering innovation.

Options to extend the number of years worked in the labor force are limited because, as discussed in Chapter 4, Koreans already remain in the labor market at much higher proportions than workers do in many other countries. The high participation rate for the elderly may be surprising, considering that South Korean retirement policies require most workers to retire at or before age 55, although the limit increased to age 60 as of 2016. The average age of Korean men leaving the labor force is 71.1, the second highest age in all OECD countries.

Because pensions and social support are minimal for the Korean elderly, many take second-career jobs that are often low-paid and/ or low-productivity, with many older workers self-employed in the agricultural or service sectors. High poverty rates coupled with limited social and familial support often results in the elderly working in the shadow economy.

RAISE POPULATION GROWTH THROUGH REUNIFICATION WITH NORTH KOREA

Although reunification with North Korea would add an additional 17.4 million potential workers in the 15–64 age range (U.S. Census Bureau 2016), Stephen (2016) has shown convincingly that reunification would probably dampen—but not solve—the elderly crisis. Using a middle series of assumptions regarding fertility and mortality, the author found that the reunified elderly population would be 16 percent lower than currently projected for South Korea in 2050 because the North Korean population is so much younger than the current South Korean population, thus resulting in a reunified population that would be somewhat younger. Although that would be a positive development, the simple addition of 17.4 million workers is not a solution in the short term because the vast majority of North Koreans would need years of education to participate in the modern economy. In addition, government spending on education for North Koreans would be in competition for additional funds needed for the South Korean elderly and pensions.

There is another potential benefit, however, of adding North Korean workers who are in their reproductive ages. As with immigrants, the workers themselves would be an addition to the labor force, but also, through a ripple effect, their children would be additional workers in the next generation. Although the total fertility rate in North Korea is estimated to be 2.0 as of 2016 and is much higher than the current 1.3 rate of South Korea (U.S. Census Bureau 2016), there is some question over whether the current levels of fertility among North Koreans would be maintained. During German reunification Eastern Germany experienced what is called a demographic shock that lowered births by 60 percent over five years (Conrad, Lechner, and Werner 1996; Goldstein and Kreyenfeld 2011). No one knows the timing of or the conditions under which reunification might happen, so it is impossible to project what might happen to fertility levels, but it is realistic to think that fertility among (former) North Koreans following reunification would not be as high as current levels. Thus, the fertility bonus may be muted.

Although it is impossible to put policies into place now for reunification of the two Koreas, planning is a key element, particularly providing education equality for all unified Koreans, a monumental task. In terms of years of education, 14 percent of North Korean men and 8 percent of females (aged 15 and over) have a tertiary education as compared with 43 percent of South Korean men and 36 percent of women aged 25–64 (Stephen 2013). Not only are the years of education at odds in the two countries, but also the quality of education, which is vastly superior in South Korea. The 2015 Programme for International Student Assessment (PISA) ranked South Korea fifth in the world for reading and math. As might be expected, little is known about the curriculum content in North Korea. In sum, we do not expect that reunification would be a large factor for short-term growth of the working-age population. Nonetheless, in the event of reunification, policies should be put in place to enhance education of the North Koreans so they could join the modern economy within a generation of reunification.

SUMMARY

The analyses above suggest the acuteness of the dilemmas that South Korea faces in trying to adopt effective social and economic policies to optimize economic growth as demographic change continues to bring declines in the size of the working-age population. Interestingly, these challenges stem from South Korea's relatively high degree of economic development on the one hand and its preservation of traditional sociocultural tendencies on the other. How is this manifest in the likely effectiveness of various policy options discussed above? In the case of fertility, the experiences of most countries in the world with post-industrial economies and low fertility suggest that efforts to increase childbearing through various incentives and social programs do not have much success in increasing birth rates. Little reason thus exists to think South Korea will be different in this regard, especially given the country's lingering commitment to Confucian family values. It does appear possible, however, that increases in female labor force participation may be attainable, especially given that room exists for change in this direction. And notably, most policy changes designed to increase fertility (better maternity leave plans, expanded and affordable childcare, improved housing affordability, and greater gender equality) are likely to exert greater boosts in female labor force participation than they are in additional births, which provides all the more reason to adopt them.

Success in increasing male labor force participation or in postponing male retirement further seems unlikely, if for no other reasons than the rates are already relatively high and Korean men already are more likely than those in other countries to hold jobs after retirement. Similarly, reunification with North Korea, given that country's appreciably lagging levels of education, at best provides the prospect of only long-term relief. By contrast, migration does offer the possibility of bolstering the size of the workforce in South Korea in the short run, as it does in the case of other advanced economy countries, but this option presents substantial integration challenges. Such obstacles are not necessarily insurmountable, but they do require countries to develop new strategies designed to accommodate newcomers, and these policies cannot be implemented overnight.

Although greater immigration may hold potential in the long run, as does reunification, solutions in the shorter term for maintaining the relative size of the workforce appear to reside mostly in efforts to increase productivity, especially by increasing education (i.e., human capital). Here again, a ceiling effect may exist for males, for whom the proportion graduating from college is already relatively quite high. But here it is not clear that room for advancement is limited. Thus, given that a substantial portion of demographic dividend benefits in general derive from education gains, and given that sustaining such gains is necessary for countries to be able to afford to transfer resources to care of the elderly, policies supporting more and better education for both males and (especially) females would appear to hold the greatest prospect for South Korea to sustain economic growth in the future.

South Korea's challenges are great, but time after time South Koreans have shown their resilience and creativity to solve societal problems. Problems associated with age restructuring will need multifaceted solutions, but I am confident that the Land of the Morning Calm will once again prevail.

REFERENCES

Abio, Gemma, Concepció Patxot, Miguel Sánchez-Romero, and Guadalupe Souto. 2017. "The Welfare State and Demographic Dividends." *Demographic Research* 36 (Article 48): 1453–1490.

Adelman, Irma. 2014. *From Aid Dependence to Aid Independence: South Korea*. eBook. 1st ed. United Nations. Accessed August 20, 2016. http://www.un.org/en/ga /second/62/iadelman.pdf.

An, Chong-Bun, Young-Jun Chun, Eul-Sik Gim, Namhui Hwang, and Sang-Hyop Lee. 2011. "Intergenerational Resource Allocation in the Republic of Korea." In *Population Aging and the Generational Economy: A Global Perspective*, edited by Ronald Lee and Andrew Mason, 381–393. Cheltenham, UK: Edward Elgar.

Anderson, Thomas M., and Hans-Peter Kohler. 2012. "Education Fever and the East Asian Fertility Puzzle: A Case Study of Low Fertility in South Korea." University of Pennsylvania PSC Working Paper Series 12-07.

Barro, Robert J. 1998. "The East Asian Tigers Have Plenty to Roar About." *Business Week*, April 24, p. 24. Accessed June 19, 2017. https://scholar.harvard.edu/barro /files/98_0427_easiantigers_bw.pdf.

Bell, Patricia A. 2004. "The Impact of Rapid Urbanization on South Korean Family Composition and the Elderly Population in South Korea." *Population Review* 43 (1): 50–60.

Bloom, David E., David Canning, and Jaypee Sevilla. 2003. *The Demographic Dividend: A New Perspective on the Economic Consequences of Population Change*. Santa Monica, CA: RAND.

Bloom, David E., and Jeffrey G. Williamson. 1997. "Demographic Transitions and Economic Miracles in Emerging Asia." NBER Working Paper 6268. Accessed June 28, 2017. http://www.nber.org/papers/w6268.

Breen, Michael. 2010. "Fall of South Korea's First President Syngman Rhee in 1960." *The Korea Times*, April 18. Accessed August 20, 2016. http://www.koreatimes.co .kr/www/news/nation/2011/01/113_64364.html.

British Broadcasting Corporation (BBC). 2012. "South Korea Opens 'Mini Capital' in Sejong City," July 2. Accessed June 15, 2017. http://www.bbc.com/news/world -asia-18670195.

Brodie, Callum. 2017. "These Are the World's Most Crowded Cities." World Economic Forum, May 22. Accessed July 26, 2017. https://www.weforum.org/agenda/2017 /05/these-are-the-world-s-most-crowded-cities/.

Casterline, John B., and John Bongaarts (eds.). 2017. *Population and Development Review* (Supplement: Fertility Transition in Sub-Saharan Africa) 43 (S1): 3–340.

Central Intelligence Agency (CIA). 2014. "The World Factbook." Accessed July 1, 2014. https://www.cia.gov/library/publications/the-world-factbook/geos/ks .html.

Chang, Kyung-Sup. 2013. "South Korea's Transition from Developmental to Post-Developmental Regime of Demographic Changes: A Perspectival Recount." Paper presented at the International Population Conference, Busan, South Korea, August 26–31.

Chew, W. Bruce. 1988. "No Nonsense Guide to Measuring Productivity." *Harvard Business Review,* January. Accessed December 19, 2016. https://hbr.org/1988/01/no -nonsense-guide-to-measuring-productivity.

Chin, Meejung, Jaerim Lee, Soyoung Lee, Seohee Son, and Miai Sung. 2012. "Family Policy in South Korea: Development, Current Status, and Challenges." *Journal of Child and Family Studies* 21: 53–64.

China Statistics Press. n.d. "Tabulation of the 2010 Census of the People's Republic of China." Accessed September 16, 2016. http://www.stats.gov.cn/tjsj/pcsj/rkpc /6rp/indexch.htm.

Cho, Uhn. 2013. "Gender Inequality and Patriarchal Order Recontextualized." In *Contemporary South Korean Society: A Critical Perspective,* edited by Hee-Yeon Cho, Lawrence Surendra, and Hyo-Je Cho, chap. 2, 18–27. London: Routledge.

Choe, Minja Kim. 2006. "Modernization, Gender Roles and Marriage Behavior in South Korea." In *Transformations in Twentieth Century Korea,* edited by Yun-Shik Chang and Steven Hugh Lee, chap. 11, 291–309. London: Routledge.

Choe, Minja Kim, and Nam-Hoon Cho. 2008. "Fertility Enhancing Population Policy in South Korea: Evolution and Prospects for Success." Paper presented at the Seminar on Fertility and Public Policies in Low Fertility Countries, Organized by the IUSSP Scientific Panel on Policies in the Context of Low Fertility, July 7–8. Barcelona: Universitat Pompeu Fabra.

Choe, Sang-Cheul, and Won-Bae Kim. 2001. "Globalization and Urbanization in the Republic of Korea." In *Facets of Globalization, International, and Local Dimensions of Development,* World Bank Discussion Paper No. 415, edited by S. Yusu, S. Everett, and J. Wei, chap. 7, 105–119. Washington, DC: World Bank.

Choe, Sang-hun. 2014. "Amid Hugs and Tears, Korean Families Divided by War Re-unite." *New York Times,* February 20. Accessed June 16, 2017. https://www.nytimes .com/2014/02/21/world/asia/north-and-south-koreans-meet-in-emotional -family-reunions.html?_r=0.

Chung, Woojin, and Monica Das Gupta. 2007. "The Role of Development and Public Policy, and the Implications for China and India." *Policy Research Working Paper* 4373. Washington, DC: World Bank. Accessed June 27, 2014. http://elibrary .worldbank.org/doi/pdf/10.1596/1813-9450-4373.

Coleman, David. 2004. "Why We Don't Have to Believe without Doubting in the 'Second Demographic Transition'—Some Agnostic Comments." *Vienna Yearbook of Population Research* 2: 11–24. Accessed November 29, 2016. http://www.jstor.org /stable/23025433.

Congressional Budget Office. 1997. "The Role of Foreign Aid in Development: South Korea and the Philippines." CBO Memorandum, Washington, DC. Accessed October 15, 2016. https://www.cbo.gov/sites/default/files/105th-congress-1997-1998 /reports/1997doc10-entire.pdf.

Connor, Phillip. 2014. "6 Facts about South Korea's Growing Christian Population." Pew Research Center. Accessed November 29, 2016. http://www.pewresearch .org/fact-tank/2014/08/12/6-facts-about-christianity-in-south-korea/.

Conrad, Christoph, Michael Lechner, and Welf Werner. 1996. "East German Fertility after Unification: Crisis or Adaptation?" *Population and Development Review* 22 (2): 331–358.

"Corporate Armistice: Can South Korea's Big and Small Companies Thrive Together?" 2013. *Economist*, October 26. http://www.economist.com/news/special -report/21588205-can-south-koreas-big-and-small-companies-thrive -together-corporate-armistice.

Crespo Cuaresma, Jesús, Wolfgang Lutz, and Warren Sanderson. 2014. "Is the Demographic Dividend an Education Dividend?" *Demography* 51: 299–315. Accessed June 22, 2017. https://link.springer.com/article/10.1007/s13524-013-0245-x.

Cumings, Bruce. 2005. *Korea's Place in the Sun: A Modern History*. New York: W.W. Norton & Company.

Cutler, David M., James M. Poterba, Louise M. Sheiner, and Lawrence H. Summers. 1990. "An Aging Society: Opportunity or Challenge?" *Brookings Papers on Economic Activity* 1. Washington, DC: Brookings Institute.

Den Boer, Andrea, and Valerie Hudson. 2017. "Patrilineality, Son Preference, and Sex Selection in South Korea and Vietnam." *Population and Development Review* 43 (1): 119–147.

Denney, Steven. 2015. "In South Korea, Changing Attitudes toward Marriage." *Diplomat*, February 27. Accessed June 19, 2015. http://thediplomat.com/2015/02/in -south-korea-changing-attitudes-toward-marriage.

Department of Statistics (Malaysia). 2015. "Vital Statistics." Accessed September 16, 2016. https://www.dosm.gov.my/v1/index.php?r=column/cthemeByCat&cat =165&bul_id=eUM5SGRBZndGUHRCZTc2RldqNGMrUTo9&menu_id=Lophe U43NWJwRWVSZklWdzQ4TlhUUTo9.

Dillon, Sam. 2008. "Elite Korean Schools, Forging Ivy League Skills." *New York Times*, April 27. Accessed September 24, 2013. http://www.nytimes.com/2008/04/27 /world/asia/27seoul.html?pagewanted=all&_r=0.

Eberstadt, Nicholas. 2011. "The Global War against Baby Girls." *The New Atlantis*. Accessed November 7, 2015. http://www.thenewatlantis.com/publications/the -global-war-against-baby-girls.

Eun, Ki-Soo. 2007. "Lowest-Low Fertility in the Republic of Korea: Causes, Consequences and Policy Responses." *Asia-Pacific Population Journal* 22 (2): 51–72.

EUROSTAT. 2016. "Population Database." Accessed September 16, 2016. http://ec .europa.eu/eurostat/web/population-demography-migration-projections /marriages-and-divorces-data.

"Farmed Out: Korean Men Are Marrying More from Choice than Necessity." 2014. *Economist*, May 24. http://www.economist.com/news/asia/21602761-korean-men -are-marrying-foreigners-more-choice-necessity-farmed-out.

"The Flight from Marriage." 2011. *Economist*, August 18. http://www.economist.com /node/21526329.

Goh-Grapes, Agnes. 2009. "Phenomenon of Wild Goose Fathers in South Korea." The *Korea Times*, February 22. Accessed September 23, 2013. http://www.koreatimes .co.kr/www/news/nation/2011/04/117_40060.html.

Goldstein, Joshua R., and Michaela Kreyenfeld. 2011. "Recent Trends in Order-Specific Fertility Dynamics." Max Planck Institute for Demographic Research Working Paper 2010-033 (revised in 2011).

Gordon, Isabel, and Jung-wha Lee. 2009. "Pensions in Australia and South Korea: A Comparative Analysis." *Pensions* 14: 273–281.

Harlan, Chico. 2012. "With New Sejong City, South Korean Government Aims to Rebalance Power." *Washington Post*, August 17. Accessed July 6, 2017. https://www.washingtonpost.com/world/asia_pacific/with-new-sejong-city-south-korean-government-aims-to-rebalance-power/2012/08/17/e8f6dc60-e2bd-11e1-a25e-15067bb31849_story.html?utm_term=.a43e6cbb0dc9.

Harper, Sarah. 2016. *How Population Change Will Transform Our World*. Oxford: Oxford University Press.

Hazzan, Dave. 2016. "Christianity and Korea: How Did the Religion Become so Apparently Prevalent in South Korea?" *The Diplomat*, April 7. http://thediplomat.com/2016/04/christianity-and-korea/.

Howe, Neil, Richard Jackson, and Keisuke Nakashima. 2007. *The Aging of Korea: Demographics and Retirement Policy in the Land of the Morning Calm*. Washington, D.C.: Center for Strategic and International Studies.

Hundt, David. 2016. "Public Opinion, Social Cohesion and the Politics of Immigration in South Korea." *Contemporary Politics* 22 (4): 1–18.

Hunt, Isabelle M., Nicola Swinson, Ben Palmer, Pauline Turnbull, Jayne Cooper, David While, Kirsten Windfuhr, Jenny Shaw, Louis Appleby, and Navneet Kapur. 2010. "Method of Suicide in the Mentally Ill: A National Clinical Survey." *Suicide and Life-Threatening Behavior* 40 (1): 22–34.

Hvistendahl, Mara. 2013. "Can China Age Gracefully? A Massive Survey Aims to Find Out." *Science* 341 (6148): 831–832. Accessed September 22, 2013. http://www.sciencemag.org/content/341/6148/831.full.

Iwulska, Aleksandra. 2012. *Golden Growth; Restoring the Lustre of the European Economic Model: Country Benchmarks*, vol. 3. Washington, DC: World Bank. Accessed May 5, 2018. http://documents.worldbank.org/curated/en/394981468251372492/pdf/681680PUB0v30G00B0x379869B00PUBLIC0.pdf.

Jeong, Insook, and J. Michael Armer. 1994. "State, Class, and Expansion of Education in South Korea: A General Model." *Comparative Education Review* 38 (4): 531–545.

Jones, Gavin. 2007. "Delayed Marriage and Very Low Fertility in Pacific Asia." *Population and Development Review* 33 (3): 453–478.

Kang, Tae-jun. 2013. "Korea's Multicultural Growing Pains." *The Diplomat*, August 20. Accessed August 20, 2017. https://thediplomat.com/2013/08/koreas-multicultural-growing-pains/.

Kang, Yewon. 2014. "Poll Shows Half of Korean Teenagers Have Suicidal Thoughts." *Wall Street Journal*, March 20. Accessed June 9, 2014. http://blogs.wsj.com/korearealtime/2014/03/20/poll-shows-half-of-korean-teenagers-have-suicidal-thoughts/.

Kelley, Allen C., and Robert M. Schmidt. 2005. "Evolution of Recent Economic-Demographic Modeling: A Synthesis." *Journal of Population Economics* 18: 275–300. Accessed June 29, 2017. http://www.jstor.org/stable/20007960.

Kim, Christine. 2015. "In South Korea Childcare Burden Derails Women's Careers." Reuters, January 27. http://www.reuters.com/article/us-southkorea-women-childcare-idUSKBN0L00B220150127.

Kim, Cynthia. 2014. "South Korea to Minimize Number of Retirees Who Launch Start-ups." Bloomberg, September 24. http://www.theglobeandmail.com/report-on-business/small-business/sb-money/cash-flow/south-korea-to-minimize-number-of-retirees-launching-startups/article20756236/.

Kim, Kyung-Hwan, and Miseon Park. 2016. "Housing Policy in the Republic of Korea." Asian Development Bank Institute [ADBI] Working Paper 570. Tokyo: ADBI. https://www.adb.org/sites/default/files/publication/183281/adbi-wp570.pdf.

Kim, Kyung-rok. 2015. "On housework, S. Korean men believe in 'fairness' . . . but don't act that way." *Hankyoreh*, December 8. Accessed August 25, 2018. http://english.hani.co.kr/arti/english_edition/e_national/720868.html.

Kim, Myong Oak, and Sam Jaffe. 2010. *The New Korea: An Inside Look at South Korea's Economic Rise*. New York: American Management Association.

Kim, Myoung-Hee, Kyunghee Jung-Choi, Hee-Jin Jun, and Ichiro Kawachi. 2010. "Socioeconomic Inequalities in Suicidal Ideation, Parasuicides, and Completed Suicides in South Korea." *Social Science and Medicine* 70: 1254–1261.

Kim, Terri. 2008. "High Education Reforms in South Korea: Public-Private Problems in Internationalising and Incorporating Universities." *Policy Futures in Education* 6 (5): 558–568.

Kim, Yoo-Ra, Kyoung Ho Choi, Youngmin Oh, Hae-Kook Lee, Yong-Sil Kweon, Chung Tai Lee, and Kyoung-Uk Lee. 2011. "Elderly Suicide Attempters by Self-Poisoning in Korea." *International Psychogeriatrics* 23 (6): 979–985.

Kim, Young-Sik. 2003. "A Brief History of the US-Korea Relations Prior to 1945." Paper presented at the University of Oregon, May 15. http://www.freerepublic.com/focus/f-news/943949/posts.

Kirk, Dudley. 1996. "Demographic Transition Theory." *Population Studies* 50: 361–387. http://shrinking.ums-riate.fr/Ressources/Chap_01/KIR_96.pdf.

Klassen, Thomas R., and Jae-jin Yang. 2010. "Introduction: Population Ageing and Income Security." In *Retirement, Work and Pensions in Ageing Korea*, edited by Jaejin Yang and Thomas R. Klassen, 1–13. London: Routledge.

Kong, Mee-Hae. 2013. "Economic Development and Women's Status." In *Contemporary South Korean Society: A Critical Perspective*, edited by Hee-Yeon Cho, Lawrence Surendra, and Hyo-Je Cho, 41–50. London: Routledge.

Koo, Se-Woong. 2015. "Anger and Envy in the Chaebol Republic." *Foreign Policy*, April 9. http://foreignpolicy.com/2015/04/09/anger-and-envy-in-the-chaebol-republic-korea-nut-rage-samsung/.

Korean Labor Institute. 2007. "Korean Longitudinal Survey of Aging, Wave 1 Questionnaire: 2006." https://g2aging.org/?section=survey&surveyid=14&display=.

"Koreans Marry Later than Ever." 2011. *Chosunilbo* (English edition), April 21. http://english.chosun.com/site/data/html_dir/2011/04/21/2011042100351.html.

Korean Statistical Information Service (KOSIS). 2013. "Population Projections by Age and Sex; Number of Incoming Foreigners by Type of Visa and Citizenship; Deaths by Cause (103 items) by Sex, by Administrative Unit; Population Density by Population Census." http://kosis.kr/eng/statisticsList/statisticsList_01List.jsp?vwcd=MT_ETITLE&parentId=A.

———. 2014. "Vital Statistics of Korea." http://kosis.kr/eng/statisticsList/statisticsList_01List.jsp#SubCont.

———. 2015. "Projected Households by Age, Type, and Size." http://kosis.kr/eng/statisticsList/statisticsList_01List.jsp?vwcd=MT_ETITLE&parentId=A#SubCont.

———. 2017. "Population Density." http://kosis.kr/eng/statisticsList/statisticsList _01List.jsp?vwcd=MT_ETITLE&parentId=A#SubCont.

Kuk, Minho. 1988. "The Government Role in the Making of Chaebol in the Industrial Development of South Korea." *Asian Perspective* 23 (1): 107–133.

Kwon, Jin-Won, Heeran Chun, and Sung-il Cho. 2009. "A Closer Look at the Increase in Suicide Rates in South Korea from 1986–2005." *BMC Public Health* 9: 72. https:// bmcpublichealth.biomedcentral.com/track/pdf/10.1186/1471-2458-9-72.

Lee, Bum Hyun. 2012. *Korean Version of New Town Development*. Supervised by Ministry of Land, Transport and Maritime Affairs (MLTM), Republic of Korea. Seoul: South Korea.

Lee, Chulhee. 2007. "Long-term Changes in the Economic Activity of Older Males in Korea." *Economic Development and Cultural Change* 56 (1): 99–123.

Lee, Jong-Wha. 2015. "How Korea Can Sustain Strong Growth." World Economic Forum. Accessed December 19, 2016. https://www.weforum.org/agenda/2015/01 /how-south-korea-can-sustain-strong-growth/.

Lee, Keun S. 1998. "Financial Crisis in Korea and IMF: Analysis and Perspectives." The Merrill Lynch Center for the Study of International Financial Services and Markets.

Lee, Myunghwa. 2015. "Legislative Initiative for Work-Family Reconciliation in South Korea: A Comparative Analysis of the South Korean, American, French, and German Family Leave Policies." *Asian American Law Journal* 22 (3): 45–104. https://scholarship.law.berkeley.edu/cgi/viewcontent.cgi?article=1210& context=aalj.

Lee, Ronald, and Andrew Mason. 2006. "What is the Demographic Dividend?" *Finance and Development* 43 (3):16–17.

———. 2013. "Population and Economic Growth in the Republic of Korea." Paper presented at the 27th International Population Conference, Busan, South Korea, August 22–31.

Lee, Sam-Sik. 2010. "Low Fertility and Policy Measures in Korea." Paper presented at the EWC-KIHASA Joint Conference on Policy Responses to Low Fertility and Aging Society, Honolulu, Hawaii, July 6–7.

Lee, Sang-Hyop, Andrew Mason, and Donghyun Park. 2012. "Overview: Why Does Population Aging Matter so Much for Asia? Population Aging, Economic Growth, and Economic Security in Asia." In *Aging Economic Growth, and Old-Age Security in Asia*, edited by Donghyun Park, Sang-Hyop Lee, and Andrew Mason, 1–31. Cheltenham, UK: Edward Elgar.

Lee, Su-Hyun. 2013. "Mom Wants You Married? So Does the State." *New York Times*, August 4. http://www.nytimes.com/2013/08/05/world/asia/mom-wants-you -married-so-does-the-state.html?_r=0.

Lee, Won Jin, Eun Shil Cha, Eun Sook Park, Kyoung Ae Kong, Jun Kyeok Yi, and Mia Son. 2009. "Deaths from Pesticide Poisoning in South Korea: Trends over 10 Years." *International Archives of Occupational and Environmental Health* 82: 365–371.

Lesthaeghe, Ron J. 2010. "The Unfolding Story of the Second Demographic Transition." *Population and Development Review* 36 (2): 211–251.

Lesthaeghe, Ron J., and Lisa Neidert. 2006. "The Second Demographic Transition in the United States: Exception or Textbook Example?" *Population and Development Review* 32 (4): 669–698. Accessed November 23, 2016. http://www.jstor.org/stable /20058923.

Lesthaeghe, Ron J., and D. J. van de Kaa. 1986. "Twee Demografische Transities?" In *Groei of Krimp* (annual book issue of "Mens en Maatschappij"), edited by R. Lesthaeghe and D. J. van de Kaa Deventer, 9–2. Netherlands: Van Loghum-Slaterus.

Library of Congress. 2013. "Guest Worker Programs: South Korea." https://www.loc.gov/law/help/guestworker/southkorea.php.

Lim, Timothy C. 2008. "Will South Korea Follow the German Experience: Democracy, the Migratory Process, and the Prospects for Permanent Immigration in Korea." *Korean Studies* 32: 28–55.

Mason, Andrew, and Ronald Lee. 2006. "Reform and support systems for the elderly in developing countries: capturing the second demographic dividend." *Genus* 67 (2): 11–35. http://u.demog.berkeley.edu/~rlee/papers/Mason%20Lee%20Genus.pdf.

McNicoll, Geoffrey. 2006. "Policy Lessons of the East Asian Demographic Transition." *Population and Development Review* 32 (1): 1–25.

Ministry of Education, Republic of Korea. 2014. "Overview." http://english.moe.go.kr/sub/info.do?m=020101&s=english.

———. 2017. "Overview." http://english.moe.go.kr/sub/info.do?m=050101&page=050101&num=1&s=english.

Ministry of Gender Equality and Family, Republic of Korea. 2016. http://www.mogef.go.kr/eng.

Ministry of the Interior, Taiwan. 2016. Gender Webpage. https://www.gender.ey.gov.tw/gecdb/Stat_Statistics_DetailData.aspx?sn=lT4902z3YmLGBZadLKLSzQ%3d%3d&d=m9ww9odNZAz2Rc5Ooj%2fwIQ%3d%3d.

Mundy, Simon. 2016. "South Korea Household Debt Pile Mounts: Burden Now Stands above 160% of Incomes as 30-Year Rise Continues." *Financial Times*, February 24. https://www.ft.com/content/f1fa1254-dad1-11e5-9ba8-3abc1e7247e4.

Noland, Marcus. 2011. "Korea's Growth Performance: Past and Future." East-West Center Working Paper 123. http://www.eastwestcenter.org/sites/default/files/private/econwp123.pdf.

———. 2014. "South Korea: The Backwater That Boomed." *Foreign Affairs* 93 (1): 17–22.

Normile, Dennis, and Mara Hvistendahl. 2012. "Making Sense of a Senseless Act." *Science* 338 (6110): 1025–1027.

Onishi, Norimitsu. 2008. "For English Studies, Koreans Say Goodbye to Dad." *New York Times*, June 8. http://www.nytimes.com/2008/06/08/world/asia/08geese.html?pagewanted=all&_r=0.

Organization for Economic Cooperation and Development (OECD). 2009. "Falling Suicide Rates in Most OECD Countries: Suicides per 100 000 Persons by Age Groups, 1960–2005." Accessed September 17, 2013. http://www.oecd-ilibrary.org/social-issues-migration-health/society-at-a-glance-2009/falling-suicide-rates-in-most-oecd-countries_soc_glance-2009-graphc04_1_-en.

———. 2011a. "Korea: Long Term Care," May 18. http://www.oecd.org/korea/47877789.pdf.

———. 2011b. "United States: Long Term Care," May 18. http://www.oecd.org/unitedstates/47902135.pdf.

———. 2012a. "Education at a Glance: OECD Indicators 2012 Korea." http://www.oecd.org/education/EAG2012%20-%20Country%20note%20-%20Korea.pdf.

———. 2012b. *OECD Economic Surveys: Korea Overview.* Paris: OECD.

———. 2013a. "PISA 2012 Results in Focus: What 15-Year-Olds Know and What They Can Do with What They Know." http://www.oecd.org/pisa/keyfindings /pisa-2012-results-overview.pdf.

———. 2013b. "Suicides." *OECD Factbook 2013: Economic, Environmental and Social Statistics.* Paris: OECD Publishing. https://www.oecd-ilibrary.org/economics/oecd -factbook-2013_factbook-2013-en.

———. 2014. "Education at a Glance: OECD Indicators, Korea Country Note." https://www.oecd.org/edu/Korea-EAG2014-Country-Note.pdf.

———. 2015. "Gender Wage Gap." https://data.oecd.org/earnwage/gender-wage -gap.htm http://www.oecd.org/gender/data/genderwagegap.htm.

———. 2016a. "Labour Force Participation Rate (indicator)." https://data.oecd.org /emp/labour-force-participation-rate.htm.

———. 2016b. *OECD Economic Surveys: South Korea.* Paris: OECD Publishing. http://www .keepeek.com/Digital-Asset-Management/oecd/economics/oecd-economic -surveys-korea-2016_eco_surveys-kor-2016-en#page15.

———. 2016c. "OECD Income Distribution Database: Data, Figures, Methods and Concepts." http://www.oecd.org/els/soc/income-distribution-database.htm.

———. 2016d. "Suicide Rates (indicator)." https://data.oecd.org/healthstat/suicide -rates.htm.

———. 2017a. "Database: Average Annual Hours Actually Worked per Worker." http://stats.oecd.org/.

———. 2017b. "GDP per Capita 2017." https://data.oecd.org/gdp/gross-domestic -product-gdp.htm).

———. 2018. "Database: Poverty Tate." https://data.oecd.org/inequality/poverty -rate.htm.

Palley, Howard A. 1992. "Social Policy and the Elderly in South Korea: Confucianism, Modernization, and Development." *Asian Survey* 32 (9): 787–801.

Park, B. C., and David Lester. 2008. "South Korea." In *Suicide in Asia: Causes and Preventions,* edited by Paul Yip, chap. 3. Hong Kong: Hong Kong University Press.

Park, Chan-Kyong. 2014. "No Easy Retirement in South Korea." *AFP,* October 22. Accessed August 29, 2018. https://www.yahoo.com/news/no-easy-retirement -south-korea-035900439.html.

Park, Chong-Min. 2009. "The Quality of Life in South Korea." *Social Indicators Research* 92 (2): 263–294.

Park, Donghyun, and Kwanho Shin. 2012. "Performance of the Service Sector in the Republic of Korea: An Empirical Investigation." Asian Development Bank Working Paper 324. Accessed December 28, 2016. https://www.adb.org/sites /default/files/publication/30081/economics-wp324.pdf.

Park, Hyunjoon. 2007. "Inequality of educational Opportunity in Korea by Gender, Socio-Economic Background, and Family Structure." *International Journal of Human Rights* 22 (1–2): 179–197.

Park, Hyunjoon, and Jaesung Choi. 2015. "Long-term Trends in Living Alone among Korean Adults: Age, Gender, and Educational Differences." *Demographic Research* 32 (43): 1177–1208. http://www.demographic-research.org/Volumes/Vol32/43/.

Park, Hyunjoon, Jae Kyung Lee, and Inkyung Jo. 2013. "Changing Relationships between Education and Marriage among Korean Women." *Korean Journal of Sociology* 47 (3): 51–76.

Park, Hyunjoon, and James M. Raymo. 2013. "Divorce in Korea: Trends and Educational Differences." *Journal of Marriage and the Family* 75 (February): 110–126.

Park, Hyunjoon, and Jeroen Smits. 2005. "Educational Assortative Mating in South Korea: Trends 1930–1998." *Research in Social Stratification and Mobility* 23: 103–127.

Park, Insook, and Lee-Jay Cho. 1995. "Confucianism and the Korea Family." *Journal of Comparative Family Studies* 26 (1): 117–134.

Park, Ju-min. 2015. "South Korean 'Superdads' on Paternity Leave Break with Tradition." Reuters, December 24. http://www.reuters.com/article/us-southkorea -superdads-idUSKBN0U626220151224.

Park, Keong-Suk. 2007. "Poverty and Inequality in Later Life: Cumulated Disadvantages from Employment to Post Retirement in South Korea." *International Journal of Sociology of the Family* 33 (1): 25–41.

Park, Yaeseul, and Elizabeth Hervey Stephen. 2013. "Is South Korea Ready for Multicultural Families ("다문화")? An Analysis of Social Media." Paper presented at the 27th International Population Conference, Busan, South Korea, August 26–30.

Phang, Hanam. 2005. "Demographic Dividend and Labour Force Transformations in Asia: The Case of the Republic of Korea." *Proceedings of the UN Expert Group Meeting on Social and Economic Implications of Changing Population Age Structures*, 119–139, Mexico City, August 31–September 2.

———. 2010. "Building Private and Occupational Pension Schemes in Korea." In *Retirement, Work and Pensions in Ageing Korea*, edited by Jae-jin Yang and Thomas R. Klassen, 96–108. London: Routledge.

Ravaneral, Zenaid R., Hwa Yung Lee, Fernando Rajulton, and Byung-Yup Cho. 1999. "Should a Second Demographic Transition Follow the First? Demographic Contrasts: Canada and South Korea." *Social Indicators Research* 47: 99–118.

Rentería, Elisenda, Guadelupe Souto, Iván Mejía-Guevara, and Concepció Patxot. 2016. "The Effect of Education on the Demographic Dividend." *Population and Development Review* 42 (4): 651–671.

Ripley, Amanda. 2011. "Teacher, Leave Those Kids Alone." *TIME* magazine, September 25. http://content.time.com/time/magazine/article/0,9171,2094427-2,00.html.

Ronald, Richard, and Hyunjeong Lee. 2012. "Housing Policy Socialization and De-Commodification in South Korea." *Journal of Housing and the Built Environment* 27: 111–131.

Scarth, William. 2002. "Population Aging, Productivity and Living Standards." In *The Review of Economic Performance and Social Progress: Towards a Social Understanding of Productivity*, edited by Andrew Sharpe, France St-Hilaire, and Keith Banting, 145–156. Montreal: Institute for Research on Public Policy.

Seth, Michael J. 2002. *Education Fever: Society, Politics, and the Pursuit of Schooling in South Korea*. Honolulu: University of Hawai'a Press.

Shin, Dong-Myeon. 2010. "The Emergence of a New Labour Market: The Changing Nature of Work and Retirement." In *Retirement, Work and Pensions in Ageing Korea*, chap. 4, 66, edited by Jae-jin Yang and Thomas R. Klassen. London: Routledge.

Shin, Eui Hang, and Keong-Suk Park. 2013. "The Compressed Development and Demographic Transition in South Korea." Paper presented at the 27th International Population Conference, Busan, South Korea, August 26–31.

Shin, Eunhye. 2012. "Getting Married in South Korea? Bring Lots of Cash." Reuters, April 27. Accessed June 19, 2015. http://www.reuters.com/article/2012/04/27/us -korea-weddings-idUSBRE83Q07Q20120427.

Shin, Jung Cheol. 2011. "Higher Education Development in Korea: Western University Ideas, Confucian Tradition, and Economic Development." *Higher Education* 64: 59–72.

Shin, Sang Do, Gil Joon Suh, Joong Eui Rhee, Joohon Sung, and Jaiyong Kim. 2004. "Epidemiologic Characteristics of Death by Poisoning in 1991–2001 in Korea." *Journal of Korean Medical Science* 19: 186–194.

Sorensen, Clark W. 1994. "Success and Education in South Korea." *Comparative Education Review* 38 (1): 10–35.

"Spate of Suicides Besieging Gangwon." 2009. *Korea Joonyang Daily*, April 24. http:// koreajoongangdaily.joins.com/news/article/article.aspx?aid=2904035.

Statistics Japan. 2015. "Statistical Handbook of Japan: 2014." http://www.stat.go.jp /english/data/handbook/c0117.htm#c02.

Statistics Korea. 2014. "The Summary Result of the 2014 Social Survey." http://kostat .go.kr/portal/eng/pressReleases/11/1/index.board?bmode=list&bSeq=&aSeq =&pageNo=2&rowNum=10&navCount=10&currPg=&sTarget=title&sTxt=.

Stephen, Elizabeth Hervey. 2013. *Demography of a Reunified Korea*. Washington, DC: Center for Strategic and International Studies.

———. 2016. "Korean Unification: A Solution to the Challenges of an Increasingly Elderly Population?" *Asian Population Studies* 12: (1): 50–67.

Stiles, Matt. 2017. "Death of K-Pop Star Shines a Spotlight on South Korea's Suicide Problem." *Los Angeles Times*, December 19. Accessed August 25, 2018. http://www .latimes.com/world/asia/la-fg-south-korea-suicide-20171219-story.html.

"Sweden 'Least Religious' Nation in Western World." 2015. *The Local*, April 13. http://www.thelocal.se/20150413/swedes-least-religious-in-western-world.

UNESCO. 2017. "Outbound Internationally Mobile Students by Host Region." http:// data.uis.unesco.org/Index.aspx?queryid=172.

United Nations. 2002. *World Urbanization Prospects: 2001*. New York: United Nations. http://www.un.org/esa/population/publications/wup2001/WUP2001_CH4 .pdf.

United Nations Databank. 2014. "Population by Age, Sex, and Urban/Rural Residence." http://data.un.org/Data.aspx?d=POP&f=tableCode%3a22%3bcountryCo de%3a410%3brefYear%3a1980%2c1985%2c1990%2c1995%2c2000%2c2005%2c2 010%2c2013&c=2,3,5,7,9,11,13,14,15&s=_countryEnglishNameOrderBy:asc,refYe ar:desc,areaCode:asc&v=41.

USAID. 2011. "Case Study. South Korea: From Aid Recipient to Donor," November 3. Washington, DC: U.S. Agency for International Development. http://photos.state .gov/libraries/korea/115197/kimnamhee/Korea%20case%20study%20 20110615%20_corrected%202020111027%20TU_%20-%2050th.pdf.

U.S. Census Bureau. 2015. "2010 Census Urban Areas FAQs." https://www.census.gov /geo/reference/ua/uafaq.html.

———. 2016. "International Population Data Base." https://www.census.gov /programs-surveys/international-programs/about/idb.html.

———. 2017. "International Population Data Base." https://www.census.gov/programs -surveys/international-programs/about/idb.html.

U.S. Library of Congress. n.d. "Country Studies: The Syngman Rhee Era, 1946–60."
http://countrystudies.us/south-korea/11.htm.

van de Kaa, D. J. 1987. "Europe's Second Demographic Transition." *Population Bulletin*
42 (1): 1–59.

"What Do You Do When You Reach the Top?" 2011. *Economist*, November 12.
http://www.economist.com/node/21538104.

Williamson, J. G. 2013. "Demographic Dividends Revisited." *Asian Development Review*
30 (2): 1–25.

World Bank. 2015. "Database." http://data.worldbank.org/indicator/SL.AGR.EMPL
.ZS?page=6.

———. 2016. "Database." http://data.worldbank.org.

———. 2017. "Database." http://databank.worldbank.org/data/reports.aspx?source
=2&series=NY.GDP.MKTP.CD.

Zagier, Alan Scher. 2012. "In South Korea, U.S. Education Means Split Families." *San
Diego Union Tribune*, April 1. http://www.sandiegouniontribune.com/sdut-in
-south-korea-us-education-means-split-families-2012apr01-story.html.

INDEX

Note: Information in figures is indicated by page numbers in italics.

ABOUT THE AUTHOR

Professor Elizabeth Hervey Stephen has been a member of the Georgetown University faculty since 1987 and has now taught well over 2,000 students. She has served in numerous administrative positions including Chair of the Department of Demography and she was the director of the Science, Technology and International Affairs Program in the Edmund A. Walsh School of Foreign Service. Prior to her appointment at Georgetown, she was a postdoctoral fellow at the Carolina Population Center, University of North Carolina, Chapel Hill; a research assistant for the Center of Population Research, University of Texas, Austin; a social science analyst for the Demographic and Behavioral Sciences Branch of the National Institute of Child Health and Human Development; a survey statistician for the U.S. Bureau of the Census; and a demographer for the Denver Regional Council of Governments. Dr. Stephen was a Fulbright Fellow for the German Studies Seminar in June 2009. She also was the recipient of a POSCO Fellowship at the East-West Center in Honolulu, Hawai'i, in 2010. She and her collaborators (Professors Victor Cha, Mike Green, Christine Kim, and Ambassador Christopher Hill) received a five-year grant from the Academy of Korean Studies for a Korean Studies Laboratory. Her recent publications on South Korea have all been a part of that grant. Dr. Stephen has been a visionary instructor and has participated in numerous pedagogy innovations that link global education with activities on the main campus. As a result of her dedication to the School of Foreign Service, in 2016 she was awarded the Constantine E. McGuire medal for her service to the school. She now teaches online courses for the main campus,

Georgetown-Qatar, and Georgetown's Villa Le Balze in Fiesole, Italy. She is the proud mother of a daughter, Anne, who is pursuing a Ph.D. in Clinical Psychology. She also serves on the Village Council of Bald Head Island, North Carolina.

ABOUT CSIS

For over 50 years, the Center for Strategic and International Studies (CSIS) has worked to develop solutions to the world's greatest policy challenges. Today, CSIS scholars are providing strategic insights and bipartisan policy solutions to help decisionmakers chart a course toward a better world.

CSIS is a nonprofit organization headquartered in Washington, D.C. The Center's 220 full-time staff and large network of affiliated scholars conduct research and analysis and develop policy initiatives that look into the future and anticipate change.

Founded at the height of the Cold War by David M. Abshire and Admiral Arleigh Burke, CSIS was dedicated to finding ways to sustain American prominence and prosperity as a force for good in the world. Since 1962, CSIS has become one of the world's preeminent international institutions focused on defense and security; regional stability; and transnational challenges ranging from energy and climate to global health and economic integration.

Thomas J. Pritzker was named chairman of the CSIS Board of Trustees in November 2015. Former U.S. deputy secretary of defense John J. Hamre has served as the Center's president and chief executive officer since 2000.

CSIS does not take specific policy positions; accordingly, all views expressed herein should be understood to be solely those of the author(s).

www.ingramcontent.com/pod-product-compliance
Lightning Source LLC
Chambersburg PA
CBHW062041270326
41929CB00014B/2499